# HOW TO BE His

*A 33-Day Dedication
to Our Eucharistic Jesus*

FR. JESSE J. MAINGOT, O.P. &
FR. IGNATIUS JOHN SCHWEITZER, O.P.
WITH DAN BURKE

SOPHIA INSTITUTE PRESS
Manchester, New Hampshire

*Imprimi potest*: Very Rev. Allen B. Moran, O.P.
March 4, 2026

*Nihil obstat*: Rev. James Brent, O.P.
March 4, 2026


Sophia Institute Press
Box 5284, Manchester, NH 03108
1-800-888-9344
www.SophiaInstitute.com

Sophia Institute Press® is a registered trademark of Sophia Institute.

paperback ISBN 979-8-88911-586-1
ebook ISBN 979-8-88911-587-8

Library of Congress Control Number: 2025945444

2nd printing

Praise for *How to Be His*

"To adore and praise God is our human obligation and privilege. To come closer to Jesus in prayer and friendship is our greatest joy. To adore Jesus in the Blessed Sacrament can change our lives. This book can help many to receive this immense grace."

—**Cardinal Anders Arborelius, O.C.D.**,
Bishop of Stockholm, Sweden

"Eucharistic revival will lead many souls to the feast of grace. But to keep them there requires internal conversion—a contemplative revolution. This book will lead you to the well where you can drink deeply of that living water that can and will bring about a profound conversion—an internal Eucharistic revival—if you will receive it."

—**Bishop Andrew H. Cozzens, S.T.D., D.D.**

"What is prayer? It is the encounter of God's thirst with ours. This book is a retreat to quench your thirst for the Truth who is Love—led by two excellent spiritual guides of the Dominican Order. Fr. Maingot and Fr. Schweitzer draw on sources "ever ancient, ever new," to elicit that amazement to which Eucharistic adoration is increasingly inviting the faithful of our day."

—**Bishop James Massa**, Rector,
St. Joseph's Seminary, Yonkers, New York

"While praying with this spiritual treasure, *How to Be His*, the words from St. John's Gospel kept welling up in my heart: 'Abide in my love' (John 15:9). Fr. Maingot and Fr. Schweitzer—relying on the wisdom of the saints—help every reader understand more deeply the Lord's desire for loving union with each one of us. I recommend this book to anyone who wants to be reminded of or come to know for the first time that Jesus is indeed here with us, loving us and healing us every day in the Eucharist."

—**Msgr. Thomas W. Powers**, Rector,
Pontifical North American College, Rome

"In *How to Be His*, Fr. Jesse and Fr. Ignatius offer a wonderful thirty-three-day series of short, deeply spiritual reflections that will, in effect, answer the question posed in the title. One cannot read this book prayerfully and walk away without realizing that "to be His" is to embrace an intense longing for Our Lord in the Eucharist. Combining essential spiritual

insights, unique perspectives of great saints, and interesting scriptural commentary, this book is an ideal entry into the practice of *lectio divina*, the slow, prayerful reading that can daily feed heart, mind, and soul."
— **Fr. Donald Haggerty**, Author, *The Hour of Testing*

"I have found that the genius of the most popular forms of prayer in the Catholic Church, such as the Rosary and Eucharistic Adoration, is that they are as accessible and efficacious for the humble neophyte or freshly converted penitent as they are for the saintly mystic. *How to Be His* shares in this genius. As a religious who has been spending an hour in Eucharistic Adoration daily for nearly twenty years, according to my institute's constitutions, I still found *How to Be His* profoundly enlightening and encouraging in my personal prayer. But I believe this book will also be fruitful for those who are just beginning to practice Eucharistic Adoration."
— **Fr. Mark-Mary Ames, C.F.R.**, Author, *Habits for Holiness*; Host, *The Rosary in a Year* podcast

"Do you want to experience or be renewed in your relationship with Jesus? The secret is in the transforming power of Jesus' love for us in the Holy Eucharist. In this book, over the course of thirty-three days, we are invited to the "Eucharistic amazement" that the saints—and above all, Mary—knew and lived. Jesus is extending an invitation to us to become truly His, and this book is a simple yet powerful guide to saying yes!"
— **Mother Amata Veritas Ellenbecker, O.P.**, Prioress General, Dominican Sisters of Mary, Mother of the Eucharist

"A very readable and inspiring book, full of truth, beauty, and goodness. Fr. Maingot and Fr. Schweitzer have given us ancient wisdom from which we can all benefit, especially in our desire to draw closer to God—who already draws close to us and awaits our response."
— **Sr. Mary Magdalene, O.P.**, Prioress, St. Dominic's Monastery, Linden, Virginia

"In *How to Be His*, Fr. Jesse Maingot and Fr. Ignatius Schweitzer lead you into the great mystery of Jesus Christ through a thirty-three-day dedication to the Holy Eucharist. Lessons of doctrine, examples of the saints, and riches from Scripture will deepen your faith in Our Lord's Eucharistic presence; they will bear fruit in your life by fostering a greater reverence for the Eucharist and a more generous service of others. That's why this book could not be timelier. While a deep narcissism in our culture keeps souls submerged in half-truths about happiness, *How to Be His* shows us that the Eucharist is not just one stimulation among others in our crowded, sensory lives. Communion in the Eucharist—whether we are at Mass or in the Adoration chapel—remains a rightly ordered work of worship, due to God in justice, that is nonetheless a work of deepest receptivity by which we receive far more than we give. Let *How to Be His* take you on this journey from a consumer mentality to a true communion mentality, so that, as Fr. Ignatius writes, you may 'enter into pure adoration of God … moving from the gifts to the Giver.'"

—**Sr. Joseph Maria, O.P.**, Prioress, Dominican
Monastery of Our Lady of the Rosary, Summit, New Jersey

"Jesus came 'to cast fire upon the earth' (Luke 12:49). *How to Be His* promises to be a powerful tool in a new stoking of that fire in these days of Eucharistic revival. It is both systematic and practical and should be welcomed by those who have lived long lives of Eucharistic Adoration as well as the many new adorers Jesus is inviting to belong to Him (or be all His). Thank you, Fr. Jesse and Fr. Ignatius!"

—**Sr. Maria of the Angels, O.P.**, Prioress,
Dominican Monastery of Our Lady of Grace,
North Guilford, Connecticut

"Fr. Jesse and Fr. Ignatius are very solid spiritual teachers, and this book is a valuable introduction to the depths of union with God that Eucharistic Adoration can lead us to."

—**Dr. Ralph Martin**, President, Renewal Ministries;
Author, *The Fulfillment of All Desire*

"Eucharistic amazement—a phrase of St. John Paul II—is an apt description of *How to Be His*. This book, born out of the authors' devotion, is overflowing with wisdom from the Scriptures, Church teaching, and the saints. If, like me, you have a deep desire for greater intimacy with Jesus, to love Him more during Mass and adoration, and to be the vessel of His love for the people you encounter daily, this book is for you. I loved every meditation."

—**Dr. Bob Schuchts**, Founder,
John Paul II Healing Center; Author, *Be Transformed*

"In a world longing for deeper meaning and relational connection, *How to Be His* is a beautiful invitation and guide to encounter Jesus personally.

Fr. Jesse Maingot and Fr. Ignatius Schweitzer bring us to the heart of the source and summit of our Faith and help us become fully alive in Christ. We highly recommend this book for anyone desiring to be brought closer to Jesus' Eucharistic presence."

—**Jake and Heather Khym**, Founders, Life Restoration Ministries; Hosts, *Restore the Glory* and *Abiding Together* podcasts

"*How to Be His* is a profound and practical treasure drawn from the rich well of the Church's wisdom. The authors invite the faithful into a deeper love for Jesus in the tabernacle—the very source and summit of the Church's mission.

"This book is a true gift to the Church, echoing Christ's words: 'I am the vine, you are the branches. He who abides in me, and I in him, he it is that bears much fruit, for apart from me you can do nothing' (John 15:5). Remaining close to Jesus in the Eucharist is the foundation of every fruitful Christian life.

"With clarity and pastoral insight, Fr. Jesse Maingot and Fr. Ignatius Schweitzer draw upon the wisdom of the saints and the light of Scripture to ignite a deeper love for Christ and His Eucharistic presence. Their work equips and strengthens readers to live their unique mission and vocation, glorifying God through thoughts, words, deeds, and actions—all flowing from an ever-growing love for Jesus, truly present, Body, Blood, Soul, and Divinity, in the Eucharist."

—**Samuel Blair**, Cofounder, *The Point Man* podcast

"This book has the power to open up your hunger for Jesus in the Eucharist. Every day of this dedication is a fresh discovery of the great gift Christ has left the Church. Fr. Jesse and Fr. Ignatius draw the reader into contact with Christ. I highly recommend this book."

—**Adam Stewart**, Executive Chairman, Sandals Resorts International

"*How to Be His* is a real eye-opener to the amazing mystery of the Eucharist and a game changer for deepening our understanding and love of our Eucharistic Lord. If you want a captivating and rich spiritual experience, this is your book."

—**Nicholas Lok-Jack**, Executive Chairman, Associated Brands Industries Limited

*To all those prayer warriors
spread throughout the world
who have committed to being hidden in prayer
before His face in Eucharistic Adoration.
Your prayer is at the source of new life
and love in the Church today.*

*The more Eucharist we receive, the more we will become like Jesus,
so that on this earth we will have a foretaste of Heaven.*

—St. Carlo Acutis


*Try basking in the sun of God's love, that is, quietly
kneeling before the Tabernacle, as you would sit enjoying the
warm sunshine, not trying to do anything, except love Him; but
realizing that, during all the time you are at His feet, more especially when dry and cold, grace is dropping down upon your soul
and you are growing fast in holiness.... Do we realise the infinite
possibilities of grace which lie hidden in the Tabernacle? Jesus
only awaits our coming; and even before we have begun
to beg His help, He has opened the treasures of His
Sacred Heart and filled our hearts with His priceless gifts.*

—Servant of God Fr. Willie Doyle, S.J.

# Contents

## Part III: Praying with Scripture

# Foreword

*How to Be His: A 33-Day Dedication to Our Eucharistic Jesus* is a timely gift to the Church. Fr. Jesse Maingot and Fr. Ignatius Schweitzer have given us more than a book: They have opened for us an immersion into Eucharistic fire. It is a pathway of love, a school of the heart, where ordinary Catholics are led more deeply into the sacred mystery of God in all His Eucharistic glory.

What I value most is how this work awakens Eucharistic desire—above all, the awareness of God's own desire for our souls. Day by day, the reader is guided through the Church's teaching, the wisdom of the saints, and the Word of God into a living encounter with Jesus in the Blessed Sacrament, the source of all renewal. It is an initiation into amazement, reverence, and love before the Real Presence.

At a time when so many have grown indifferent to this mystery, *How to Be His* is a clarion call back to the heart of our Faith. It teaches us to linger with Christ, to recognize His gaze upon us, and to be transformed into His likeness. For those seeking to grow in holiness, and for families and communities longing to revive their faith, this book offers a sure and proven pathway.

I am grateful for this work. It will rekindle Eucharistic devotion in the Church and, through that devotion, bring about the renewal our world so urgently needs.

—✝ Charles Jason Gordon
Archbishop of Port of Spain

# How to Get the Most from This Book

Why is this book in your hands? There are shallow answers to this question that begin and end on a human dimension. A deeper understanding comes through the lens of God's sovereignty—that God allows or causes all things. From this vantage point, we know that this book is in your hands because God desired it. Why and for what purpose? Does that mean that you fulfill your duty by simply reading it, as you might any book? Is it the extent of God's will that you acquire new and good ideas about the Eucharist?

I don't think you believe that, and neither do I. While I am sure that this book is in your hands because God willed it, I am also sure that it is for a far greater purpose than just to increase your intellectual knowledge. The reason for my certainty is both because of sound theology regarding God's will[1] and because I believe this book is very special. The perspective provided here can and will change your life for the better—*if* you engage it in

---

[1] See Dan Burke, *Finding Peace in the Storm: Reflections on St. Alphonsus Ligouri's Uniformity with God's Will* (Sophia Institute Press, 2023).

a way that allows the wisdom to move beyond your intellect to your heart.

Saints know this pathway very well—head to heart. In fact, the reason they are saints is because they understand what it means to encounter God and to yield to His presence in and through what others might see as mundane—like reading a book. Saints read books differently than everyone else, and this is one of the many reasons they become saints. How is this?

First, they have a clear understanding of what we have already asserted—God is present and working in and through every circumstance. Second, and this is the most important point, they embrace and receive Him in and through every circumstance. They don't read like everyone else reads. Instead, they encounter God in their reading.

Of course, this raises an important question: "Well, if I am not a saint, can I read the way they read?" The answer is, you can, and here are three essential "ingredients" for fruitful reading.

**Sacred time:** First, set aside sacred time. Sacred time is that time that you strive eagerly to give to God alone. What does that mean? Well, for example, you might determine that you need at least fifteen minutes a day in order to give this encounter more room to work in you, to really give yourself to this sacred reading. In order to do that, you may need to get up a half hour earlier than normal. Striving for this sacred time can be the game-changer in your spiritual life. You could ask a friend to hold you accountable to this time. This accountability can help us to keep our commitment to this sacred encounter even when we don't feel like it. Just know that when we make time sacred—set aside only for God—we invite God into this time. This is an invitation God never refuses.

**Sacred space:** As a sign that you are about to keep your commitment to God to spend sacred time with Him, take this book to a place that is conducive to helping you draw near to God—that is, a sacred space that is dedicated to prayer and the worship of God. Sacred spaces always have images and other decorations that help to draw our hearts to the reality that we are in God's presence as we read and pray. You can make a sacred space in your home with something as simple as an icon and a candle. Even better, take this book each day until you finish it to an adoration chapel or church to meet the Lord in the Blessed Sacrament. Regardless of which sacred space you prefer, be sure it is a space clearly dedicated to God's presence and used for nothing else. This will help you focus better.

**Sacred attention:** There are two aspects of sacred attention. The first is that it always begins with invoking or recognizing the presence of God. How do saints invoke the presence of God? There is a simple yet powerful prayer that God *always* answers; it is thousands of years old and prayed by untold numbers of saints. "O God, come to my assistance; O Lord, make haste to help me" (Ps. 69:2, DRA). This prayer, of course, assumes something about the posture of the soul who begins to read. That is, they are reading in and through the presence of God.

The second aspect of sacred attention follows an ancient pattern revealed by a holy Carthusian monk named Guigo. He outlined four powerful ways you can discover God in sacred reading:

1. **Read:** Avoid reading sacred ideas the way you read everything else. If you treat sacred ideas like banal ideas, they will become, to you, banal. If you treat sacred ideas as if they are sacred, the power within them will emerge in you. How do you do this? Simply

begin reading slowly and even out loud (as long as you are doing so in private). When you pray aloud, you are more present to the words and the ideas and thus to the God who seeks to meet you in them. Read with the desire to meet God—slowly, attentively, and prayerfully.

2.  **Reflect**: Make an effort to engage prayerfully with the meaning of the passage and to consider how it may apply to your life circumstances. It may be helpful to consider the ideas as if you were in the scene of the passage, or as if God was revealing the content to you in order specifically to teach you how to know and become one with Him.

3.  **Respond**: As you encounter ideas and they become relevant to you, it is important that you speak with Him about them. If you are in awe, share that with the Lord. If you don't understand, ask Him to reveal more to you to help you understand.

4.  **Rest**: When you come to a passage in this book that causes something to move in you, stop reading and rest. This stage is extremely important. When God moves, you must yield and allow Him to move in you. Allow yourself to rest and remain absorbed in the wisdom and presence of God, allowing or inviting the Holy Spirit to draw you more deeply into His presence through what you've read. Don't grasp at the experience, just let it come. If it brings tears, let them flow. Whatever the experience, just allow it to play out in you. Once it fades, return to the passage that impacted you and reread it. Do this over and over until there is no longer any movement. By the way, don't worry

if there is nothing to experience at all. Just give your heart and mind to the text and trust that the Lord is working even if you don't experience anything.

5.  **Resolve**: This is the phase where you ensure that you are not just accumulating ideas for the sake of ideas. St. Paul reveals that this kind of knowledge "puffs up" but love "builds up." When we truly encounter God, our love increases and naturally spills out on others. If this is not happening, seek out a spiritual director to help you dig into why your knowledge is limited to ideas rather than being an encounter with Jesus Himself. At each encounter, ask yourself: "How should this reading change how I interact with God and those He has placed in my care?" The questions we provide at the end of each chapter should be a great launching point for either deeper reflection or entering more fully into how to truly be transformed by what you are reading.

Assuming your foundational approach looks something like this path of Divine Reading (*Lectio Divina*), the final and most powerful way to approach this book is to share it with others. This does *not* mean you need to know how to teach what you will learn in this book. We have provided special video resources that you can access and share, free of charge, at https://spiritualdirection.com/His. We wanted to make it as easy as possible for everyone—this means you too—can get a group of Catholics together on a regular basis and read together and answer and discuss the questions at the end of each chapter. As you share with others, all that you have personally gained in your efforts will be magnified in you and in others.

The Holy Spirit in the book of James reveals that if you draw near to God, He will draw near to you. This passage is both a command and a promise. You were made to draw near—you are called to draw near; you are equipped to draw near; you must draw near—in order to become the saint that God has destined you to become. If you do that, this book will lead you to know Him in ways you never would have imagined possible. May you answer the call, and may Jesus Christ be praised.

Dan Burke
President, Avila Foundation
for Spiritual Formation

# Introduction

*I keep the LORD always before me;*
*because he is at my right hand, I shall not be moved. . . .*
*Thou dost show me the path of life;*
*in thy presence there is fulness of joy,*
*in thy right hand are pleasures for evermore.*

—Psalm 16:8, 11

There is such a thing as Eucharistic fire. It is the burning love of the Eucharistic Jesus that sets our hearts aflame. It is a fire of joy and happiness in His presence. It is a radiant light that burns away our sinful tendencies, our worries, our despair, and our insecurity. It is a fire of strength and power to endure the crosses of life. It never fails to amaze me how transformative it is to be with Jesus. No one ever comes to Jesus with an open heart and leaves unchanged. Many years ago, when I had just reverted back to my Catholic Faith, a friend explained that sitting in front of the tabernacle or monstrance changes the soul simply by being there. Jesus shines forth His grace and life, making the soul radiant with light. My friend said it was like sitting in the sun and receiving a tan. You simply have to put yourself there, and the sun does all the work. Dear reader, put yourself in Jesus' presence, and His presence alive and active will transform you more into Himself. You will learn how to be His.

My own experience of adoration and lingering in His presence is the root of my own conviction that the antidote to our problems is to simply be with Christ. As a priest I (Fr. Jesse) am privileged to speak to countless people in many different situations who witness to the power of being with Jesus. Listening to so many situations, I am convinced that being with Jesus' true presence is the most practical thing we can do for changing the world. It is how we become vessels of grace for the salvation of souls. Spending time with Jesus has a hidden but powerful effect on the whole of humanity. One of the most striking descriptions of the effect of adoration I have ever read was written by the renowned theologian and philosopher Peter Kreeft:

> Restoration of adoration of the Sacrament will heal our church, and thus our nation, and thus our world. It is one of Satan's most destructive lies that sitting alone in a dark church adoring Christ is irrelevant, impractical, a withdrawal from vital contemporary needs. Adoration touches everyone and everything in the world because it touches the Creator, who touches everything and everyone in the world from within, in fact, from their very center. When we adore, we plunge into the center of the hurricane, "the still point of the turning world"; we plug into infinite dynamism and power. Adoration is more powerful for construction than nuclear bombs for destruction.[2]

---

[2] Peter Kreeft, *The Angel and the Ants: Bringing Heaven Closer to Your Daily Life* (Servant Publications, 1994), 92

Kreeft is right. Adoration releases power from on high. It is the most constructive activity we can partake in for the Kingdom. There is an immense power that flows out of the Lord in His Real Presence when He is touched by faith. "Some one touched me; for I perceive that power has gone forth from me" (Luke 8:46). The Lord goes on to tell the woman who touched Him that it was faith that drew power from Him. With faith you and I can be that same person who touched Jesus. The truth is, when we touch Jesus in adoration, power flows not only into our life but through us into the whole Church.

How many marriages have been saved because people went to Jesus, and He gave them peace and new love? How many vocations to religious life and priesthood have been renewed before the gaze of Jesus from the Eucharist? How many diseases and how much mental illness have been healed when Jesus radiated His love? Even when Jesus has not healed for reasons known only to His wisdom, how many people have received strength and joy to carry their cross?

People tell me they have received ideas for business opportunities in front of Jesus. Some have received inspirations to make new developments in science and even politics. Some have received new ideas of developing organizations that help make the world a better place. So many have found the cure to their addictions and other moral problems by simply being with Jesus. During the beginning of the pandemic, churches were forced to close. A nurse said to my superior, Fr. John, that she was distraught because sitting before Jesus was the sole source of her strength to deal with the sick in the hospital all day. It made her alert and filled her with hope and love. The list is endless. The point is simple: Visiting Jesus has real consequences on lives and the world around us. Being with Jesus saves souls.

The point of this dedication is to help contribute to a Eucharistic revival in our own hearts and in the Church. It is to bring about a greater release of grace and power from the Lord to transform our times. Let us now turn to the concept of dedication.

## What Is This Dedication?

We have titled this book *How to Be His* because it captures what the whole Christian spiritual life is about. To belong to Christ is the goal of every disciple of Jesus. We are not meant only to imitate Jesus' life; we are called to grow in union with Him more and more. The sacramental life is the means by which Jesus has chosen to communicate His supernatural life of grace to us. Baptism plunges us into this life, Confession renews it when it is lost or when it is weakened, Confirmation strengthens it to empower us, marriage makes it visible in the way Jesus loves the Church, priesthood makes it available for us all, Anointing of the Sick empowers the soul with healing and also the strength to pass into the next life, and the Eucharist, Jesus Himself, is the source and summit of this life. If we speak about belonging to Jesus, what begins in Baptism is perfected and nurtured and transformed by the Eucharistic Jesus. This transformation happens through receiving Jesus in Holy Communion. It also happens in faithful adoration of Jesus in the celebration of Holy Mass and in the adoration of Jesus in the tabernacle or Jesus exposed in the monstrance. Our Eucharistic Lord is the principal means by which we become His. This thirty-three-day dedication aims to help us in our journey to growing in union with Jesus Christ. Such a journey is always about love. It is about growing in love of Jesus, a love which is also the fruit of meditation, a love that sends us out to love and call others to love Him in the way that He deserves.

All baptized souls have already been consecrated to Christ. Because of this, when thinking about this book, I decided to choose the word *dedication* rather than *consecration*. Maybe in theory there is not much of a difference, depending on one's definition of these terms. When we speak of dedication to the Eucharistic Lord, we mean binding and giving ourselves to Jesus in the way that He comes to us in the Eucharist. Our dedication is an intentional holy resolution to reform our lives in view of the Eucharist. It is a commitment to endeavor to grow in love of Holy Mass and to learn to "waste time" with the Lord in adoration of the Host, giving our Eucharistic Lord more and more of our free time. Believing in how constructive and efficacious adoration is for the world, within Mass and outside of Mass we dedicate ourselves to become agents of great grace for the salvation of souls and the transformation of the world. We pray that in the process we too shall be ever more sanctified.

Now, this dedication is not only about a commitment to Eucharistic Adoration. It is also about promising to be agents of change in Eucharistic worship and adoration culture in the Church. If you agree to do this thirty-three-day preparation for a dedication to the Eucharistic Lord, it means you want to become intentional about building up an atmosphere in our churches, chapels, and even our everyday lives, which all points to the Lord of all glory present in the Eucharist. It means you want to see the Lord exposed and adored perpetually in all parishes and Christian communities of the world, and that you will pray for this Eucharistic reign of Jesus Christ.

Why is this needed? Sadly, a lot of Catholics have forgotten about Jesus in the tabernacle or have never really learned how to be with Jesus in His Eucharistic presence. Many have a superficial understanding of the Eucharistic mystery. Quite a lot of Catholics do not even believe that the Eucharist is truly the Body and Blood, soul and divinity of Jesus Christ. Even for us who do believe, it is a spiritual struggle to fight our sleepy flesh to keep alert to the truth of the Eucharist. It is easy to be casual in attending the Holy Sacrifice of the Mass. We do not always see it as the most important time of the day or week. As priests, we can also become routinized and feel banal in the celebration of the liturgy. The way we as priests handle the Lord in Mass or exposition can give signals to the faithful of our own lack of faith in the Eucharist. This in turn can also negatively shape and affect the reverence and faith of the laity.

Throughout the whole Church, we often see examples of irreverent behavior in churches, such as people speaking loudly and having conversations that should happen outside, chatting with each other in the church as if the Lord is not present. When we approach the altar, many hearts are cold and indifferent. So often we have not prepared well for Mass and for Holy Communion. Our awareness of the need to linger in thanksgiving after Mass is virtually nonexistent in many churches. So many pass by a church and do not enter to spend time with Jesus who waits for them in the tabernacle. Many parishes are fortunate to have Eucharistic Adoration; however, Jesus is exposed and so few go to be with Him. The list goes on and on.

The bottom line is that the Catholic culture around worship and adoration needs to be rebuilt. The temple is in ruins. We need to rebuild an atmosphere of Eucharistic awe and reverence. Pope St. John Paul II called it "Eucharistic 'amazement.'"[3] We need to start living with the deep awareness that the Lord of

---

[3] Pope John Paul II, Encyclical Letter on the Eucharist *Ecclesia de Eucharistia* (April 17, 2003), no. 6.

Lords and King of Kings dwells in His glorified flesh on earth while in Heaven. A renewal of attitudes and behavior around the Eucharist is greatly needed. This dedication aims at committing ourselves to propagating this renewal. Of course it begins in our own hearts. We have to first be convicted that the Eucharist is the same Jesus we read about in the Gospels. I myself have been guilty of many of the things I have listed. I hope that by this "retreat" we can all make reparation for past mistakes with a resolve to give Jesus the time, reverence, love, and adoration that He is all-worthy of receiving.

## The Plan of These Weeks

We want to fall more in love with Jesus in the Eucharist. We want to grow in a keen awareness of His radiant Eucharistic face. This will help strengthen our resolve in our dedication to be with Him more and to build up a culture of Eucharistic amazement. A very helpful principle in Dominican spirituality is that knowledge is indispensable for love. We cannot love what we do not know. Therefore, over the first eleven days, I (Fr. Jesse) will plumb some of the richness of the Church's teaching on the Eucharist in order to try to uncover the deeper meaning of the Eucharist in the overall plan of salvation. This book is not meant to be a theological treatise on the Holy Sacrifice of the Mass. Nevertheless, we cannot separate the Holy Eucharist from the celebration of the Eucharist. This book, however, focuses on Eucharistic Adoration.

After this, Fr. Ignatius and I will spend eleven days diving into the lives and wisdom of saints whose hearts burned with Eucharistic fire; my reflections are found on days 12–18, and Fr. Ignatius's reflections are on days 19–22. The hope is that we can all catch the scent of their Eucharistic love. May the anointing on their lives and words inspire us to greater dedication to the Holy Eucharist.

Finally, after spending some time with the saints, for the final eleven days we will ponder the Eucharistic mystery in the light of Sacred Scripture. Fr. Ignatius will help us unpack the treasure chest of God's Word in these days. The soul of theology is the Word of God. It is fitting that we therefore drink from the source of revelation to help us make our journey to dedication. May God's radiant word pierce our hearts with greater longing to belong to the Eucharistic Lord.

I hope that, together, these sources of wisdom and knowledge will bring about a deeper love for Jesus in the tabernacle. We can know many truths of our faith in a superficial way. However, if we spend a long time on one mystery-truth from many angles, such a truth has a greater chance of becoming real in our hearts. As they say, there is a long journey from the head to the heart. It is one thing for us to know doctrine and truths of our faith and another for them to be deeply felt truths alive in us. The mind and the heart must be united. Part of the plan of these coming weeks is to *pray* these thirty-three days rather than simply *read* them. Prayerful meditation gives birth to conviction, and conviction brings depth and interiority. It brings passion and zeal. What the Church needs above all is a contemplative revolution around the Eucharistic Jesus which brings about true experiential knowledge of Jesus. I am convinced that Eucharistic devotion and sanctity will renew the Church and that such renewal of holiness is our greatest evangelization. Fr. Ignatius and I hope this book can be used by the Lord to contribute to this contemplative revolution.

I'll end this section by quoting a powerful and simple reflection from a document of the Holy See addressed to religious (those men and women who have chosen to live a consecrated life shaped by the evangelical counsels of poverty, chastity, and obedience). While the document addresses religious, the statement can be equally valuable and inspiring to those in all states of life in the Church. The document can challenge all Christians to the contemplative life.

> The contemplative dimension is the real secret of renewal for every religious life. It vitally renews the following of Christ because it leads to an experiential knowledge of him. This knowledge is needed for the authentic witness to him by those who have heard him, have seen him with their own eyes, have contemplated him, and have touched him with their own hands (cf. 1 Jn 1:1; Philip 3:8).[4]

All I can say is, what greater experiential knowledge of Jesus do we have, what greater way to hear, see, contemplate and touch Him, than in the Eucharist? What greater experience of Jesus Christ can we have in this life than to be actually with Him in His Eucharistic form? Of course, as St. Thomas Aquinas says of the Eucharist, "Faith alone sees his face."

Lastly …

As is said, save the best for last. Novenas of Masses, Holy Hours, Rosaries, have been offered for those who read and complete the journey laid out in this book. May the Lord bless you with all these prayers offered for you. He knows each one of us

---

[4]  Eduardo Cardinal Pironio and Augustine Mayer, O.S.B., *The Contemplative Dimension of Religious Life* (Plenoria of the Sacred Congregation for Religious and for Secular Institutes, March 4–7, 1980), no. 30, https://www.vatican.va/roman_curia/congregations/ccscrlife/documents/rc_con_ccscrlife_doc_12081980_the-contemplative-dimension-of-religious-life_en.html.

and is faithful to our prayers. We can be confident that we will receive the blessings of all these prayers. Let us proceed, confident in the words of our Lord Jesus Christ: "What father among you, if his son asks for a fish, will instead of a fish give him a serpent; or if he asks for an egg, will give him a scorpion? If you then, who are evil, know how to give good gifts to your children, how much more will the heavenly Father give the Holy Spirit to those who ask him!" (Luke 11:11–13).

Come, Holy Spirit!

Fr. Jesse Maingot, O.P.
Feast of the Presentation of the Lord
February 2025

Part I

# The Church's Teachings on the Eucharist

The doctrines of the Church, given to her by Christ, are not just facts; they are true initiations of the mind and heart into the very mystery of God. This initiation is a real contact with the living God Himself. Catholic doctrines are like guardians of mystery, guiding our minds to come to a true knowledge of the Lord.

In these first eleven days of our thirty-three-day journey, we are not only learning doctrines about the Holy Eucharist, we are truly encountering the Lord in and through them. We are gathering sacred knowledge to deepen our love for our Eucharistic Lord. It is important to note that the next few days are not exhaustive teachings on the Holy Eucharist. The goal is simply to situate the gift of our Eucharistic Lord within the wider context of the mystery of salvation. The goal is to appreciate how the Holy Eucharist is an answer to the question: "How to be His?"

Day 1

# God Longs for Us

*My beloved is mine and I am his.*

—Song of Solomon 2:16

Dear Reader,

If you have not yet done so, please read the introduction before you begin these daily meditations. It is crucial to understanding the purpose of this preparation for dedication.

Lost in our own search for God, we can forget that our Lord and God has a passionate love for each one of us. He longs for us. We must begin these weeks of preparation convinced of this. One of the best texts that I have seen that so clearly spells out this great truth of God's longing for us is found in the *Catechism of the Catholic Church* (CCC) on prayer. Using Jesus' conversation with the Samaritan woman at the well as a reference (John 4:1–15), the *Catechism* says:

> The wonder of prayer is revealed beside the well where we come seeking water: there, Christ comes to meet every human being. It is he who first seeks us and asks us for a drink. Jesus thirsts; his asking arises from the depths of

God's desire for us. Whether we realize it or not, prayer is the encounter of God's thirst with ours. God thirsts that we may thirst for him. (no. 2560)

These sentiments are echoed in St. Teresa of Avilas's *The Interior Castle*. The great mystic and doctor of the Church says that "this Beloved of ours is merciful and good. . . . He so deeply longs for our love that He keeps calling us to come closer."

Another Teresa, St. Mother Teresa of Calcutta, heard in her heart the words "I thirst" (John 19:28), the intense longing of Jesus on the Cross for our souls. The Cross reveals to us the great thirst of God. This is the same as saying we are pursued by God. It is a beautiful perspective to see our spiritual life as pursued by divine love, to see it as a time of grace to be captured by the Lord, to become His.

The way we are captured is by drawing close to Jesus Christ, who remains with us by means of the Eucharist. The Eucharistic Jesus waits to give us every blessing and grace to make us more closely united with Him. He waits in the Eucharist to burn into our hearts a deeper love for the Holy Trinity. Jesus is the door that opens us into the heavenly realms of grace beyond our wildest imagination and senses. It is important to remember our Heavenly Father in this process of becoming more intimate with Jesus. The Scriptures tell us that God the Father is constantly drawing us to His Son: "No one can come to me unless the Father who sent me draws him" (John 6:44). He draws us to His Son to draw us to Himself, because when we come close to Jesus we come close to the Father because They are one: "He who has seen me has seen the Father; how can you say, 'Show us the Father'?" (John 14:9). I believe this book in your hands is one among many means by which the Father is calling you.

This thirty-three-day dedication is about learning how to let ourselves be captured more and more by the Lord. To do this we have first to be convinced that He desires us. It is important to be aware of this from the beginning of these days of preparation for dedication. Let us cultivate a sense of awe and wander that the Lord is calling us to a deeper intimacy with Him. Let it settle into your bones that your deep desire for the Lord is really His desire for you. Our love for Him is always His love poured out in our hearts first. Our pursuit of Him is really His pursuit of us. Your deepening desire for Jesus could only ever be a grace from Him. It is true that you can freely reject this desire, but let yourself be drawn to Him. If you have a desire in your heart for Jesus and if you want to dedicate yourself to Him more completely, then this is a sure sign the Father is calling you to Himself in a deeper way. Pause and let this truth sink into your heart.

When this truth resonates not only in our minds but also in our hearts, we will desire to be with Jesus more and more. Pope St. John Paul II once said that it is hard for us to love those people who do not desire us. Mutual desire builds true friendship. The truth is, we all experience people in our lives who are often inconsistent in their love for us. At times we may even feel abandoned by them or undesired by them. Thankfully, Jesus loves and longs for you with a perfect, infinite love. He never stops. He is ever constant and faithful: "O give thanks to the Lord, for he is good, for his steadfast love endures for ever" (Ps. 136). His love has the power to stir in us an ever-growing response of love. His love is the true key to unlock untold depths in our own heart.

Where else can we find Him so tangibly than in the Eucharist? As we will see these coming days, it is principally through the Eucharist that Jesus makes us His own more and more. It is at his feet in the tabernacle that we can hear with faith the great longing of His heart for our love.

*Let Us Pray:* Lord, I want every part of my heart and my life to belong to You. Please remove all obstacles that prevent me from becoming one with You.

## Today's Reflection

*What line or passage caught your attention as you read?*

*When Fr. Jesse observed that Jesus "longs
for us," how did you respond?*

*Have you considered that your desire for the Lord
is really Him drawing you to Himself?*

If you are able, spend some time today with Jesus in His Eucharistic presence. Ask Him to give you the grace of longing.

Day 2

# Becoming His

*I have been crucified with Christ; it is no longer*
*I who live, but Christ who lives in me.*

—Galatians 2:20

The passionate love of the Lord for us is so marvelous that the
Lord does not only want to draw us to Himself, He wants to
draw us *into* Himself. This is the deeper meaning of how we
become His: a Christian is one who is caught and transformed
in divine love.

So, how are we caught? How do we become His? It is through
Baptism. Baptism plunges us into Jesus' life. It unites us to Him
by the power of the grace of the Holy Spirit. The Holy Spirit
communicates to the baptized the very life of Jesus. A life that
Jesus received from His Father in all eternity, an eternal life. The
Christian is no longer a child of God only on the level of creation;
he or she becomes a child in the order of grace. This is why the
Lord has commanded us: "Go therefore and make disciples of
all nations, baptizing them in the name of the Father and of the
Son and of the Holy Spirit" (Matt. 28:19).

Dom Paul Delatte, an abbot of the famous Solesmes monastery in France, said that all our Christian life can be summed up in these words: "how to inherit." Those words have always stayed with me. They have made me see my faith from a different perspective. We are inheritors of the very intimate life of the Holy Trinity which comes to us through Christ. It can only be Christ, because He is the eternal inheritor of everything that the Father *is* and gives. The Nicene Creed professes: Jesus is "born of the Father before all ages. God from God, Light from Light, true God from true God, begotten not made, consubstantial with the Father."

When we speak of Jesus' very identity as Son of God, we mean precisely what the Nicene Creed professes: that Jesus is "God from God, Light from Light." Christianity is a supernatural and mystical participation in this eternal coming forth from the Father, which we call the sonship of Christ. It is a sharing in the very divine light and life that Christ receives from His Father. This sharing is made possible only through Baptism. Through Baptism, what is Jesus' is now mine: His life is my own. It is not an exaggeration to say that we "become Jesus" in Baptism because such is the union between him and us. This is the gospel, the good news.

Bl. Columba Marmion, in his book *Christ the Life of the Soul*, opens up for us the deeper mystery of this inheritance. He emphasizes that Christianity is more than just an imitation of Christ; it is about Jesus reproducing His life in us. It is about Christ being the very life of our souls. This is why St. Paul could pray: "I have been crucified with Christ; it is no longer I who live, but Christ who lives in me" (Gal. 2:20).

Do we really understand the dignity of being baptized into Jesus? We are not just imitators of Christ but true sons and daughters of the Father because we share in the life of the Eternal Son. St. Elizabeth of the Trinity, a contemporary of St. Thérèse of

Lisieux, came to know the depths of the mystical reality of Jesus living in us. The Carmelite nun prayed,

> O Consuming Fire, Spirit of Love,
> Overshadow me so that the Word may be,
> As it were incarnate again in my soul.
> May I be for him a new humanity in which
> He can renew all his mystery.[5]

Isn't that amazing? Jesus wants to renew his whole life through you and me.

How does Jesus renew and deepen His whole mysterious life in us? It is primarily by the Holy Mass and consuming and adoring the Eucharistic Jesus. The life of Jesus which begins in us in Baptism must be nurtured and deepened by partaking of the Eucharistic Jesus. Jesus instituted the Eucharist as a way of giving Himself as food for the journey to Heaven. When we receive Jesus in Holy Communion, He comes with power to transform us into Himself. This is a truth we will expound on more tomorrow.

It is also true that when we adore Jesus in the Eucharist outside of Mass (in the tabernacle or monstrance), we are drawn more deeply into the heart of Christ. Eucharistic Adoration is a spiritual communion with the Lord. It is the repeated experience of so many Catholics that, in Eucharistic Adoration, the Eucharistic Jesus helps uncover our truest and most noble desires. When we are before His sacred presence, He declutters our hearts from so many lies. All that is not true collapses under His light. The truth

---

[5] See "The Trinitarian Prayer of St. Elizabeth of the Trinity" (excerpted and format adapted), St. Elizabeth of the Trinity Secular Discalced Carmelites of Tulsa, https://www.ocdstulsa.com /prayer-of-st-elizabeth-of-the-trinity/.

of who we are in Him surfaces. In His gentle presence, shame melts away and the conviction of His goodness is born anew in our hearts. He returns us to true selves. St Elizabeth of the Trinity says it like this: "We shall not be purified by looking at our miseries, but by gazing on Him who is all purity and holiness." It is by gazing at Jesus that our hearts become pure and true. We become His.

> *Let Us Pray:* Lord, help me become aware that Christ has no body on earth but mine, no hands, no feet on earth but mine. Jesus, use my eyes to look with compassion upon others. May my feet be your feet, bringing good news. Use my hands to bless the world. Lord, increase in me a desire to be docile to your voice. Transform me into you more and more. (Adapted from the prayer attributed to St. Teresa of Avila.)

## Today's Reflection

*"A Christian is one caught and transformed in divine love." How have you experienced this?*

*"We are inheritors of the intimate life of the Holy Trinity." What does this mean for you?*

*Is our Christian life only about morality? Is there something more to being called a Christian?*

Day 3

# Transformed in Him

*What material food produces in our bodily life, Holy
Communion wonderfully achieves in our spiritual life.
Communion with the flesh of the risen Christ ... preserves,
increases, and renews the life of grace received at Baptism.*

—Catechism of the Catholic Church,
no. 1392 (emphasis added)

These days we are reflecting on how the Lord longs for us with a passionate love. We have seen that this longing for us is so intense that the Lord wants to make us part of Him. This is because God is love and love seeks union always with the one being loved.

In his book *Fire and Light: Learning to Receive the Gift of God*, Fr. Jacques Philippe says that it is in the Eucharist that "the mad dream of all lovers is realized: to be one in being with the object of our love."[6] Yesterday we saw that Baptism creates this union with God through adoption in Jesus Christ. Today we reflect on how the mystery of the Eucharist is the deepening and perfection

6   Fr. Jacques Philippe, *Fire and Light: Learning to Receive the Gift of God* (Scepter, 2016), 111.

of this union with Christ. A transformation wrought in the fire of divine love.

In Holy Mass, Jesus acting through the priest transforms bread and wine into Himself so that we can receive Him completely in Holy Communion. It is always good for us to remember that we do not receive stuff, or just the presence of Jesus' Body and Blood as if it is in a container called the Eucharist. No, we receive a person, the Divine Person of Jesus Christ. The Eucharist is not an "it" but a "Him." Accenting this understanding brings out the intimacy of love that is Holy Communion. It is a person-to-person encounter of love. As a priest, I always try to celebrate Holy Mass, reminding and telling myself that I am holding the living God in my hands when I hold the Host. I often think of these words of St. Francis of Assisi: "Let the entire man be seized with fear; let the whole world tremble; let Heaven exult when Christ, the Son of the Living God, is on the altar in the hands of the priest."[7] These words also challenge me to keep my mind and heart on the fact that I am entrusting the living God to His people at Communion time. How incredible is this mystery of faith?

It is good for us to have awe and wonder over the fact that when we receive the Body and Blood of Christ we also receive Jesus' soul and divinity as well. In his book *The Eucharist and the Trinity* (also published as *From the Eucharist to the Trinity*), Fr. Marie Vincent Bernadot, O.P., a renowned French Dominican preacher and retreat master, comments that at Communion time we have "within us the incarnate Word, with all He is and with all He does. We have Jesus-both God and man, all the treasures of His

---

[7] St. Francis of Assisi, *The Writings of St. Francis of Assisi*, trans. by Pascal Robinson (Dolphin Press, 1905), 115.

divinity, and all the graces of His humanity. In our possession are, in St. Paul's terms, 'the unsearchable riches of Christ' (Eph. 3:8)."[8]

These unsearchable riches of Christ flow from Jesus' divinity into His sacred humanity. Therefore, contact with Jesus' flesh is a mysterious contact with His divinity. Who can come into contact with this divine flesh and remain the same? St. John Paul II puts it like this: "The most holy Eucharist contains the Church's entire spiritual wealth: Christ himself, our passover and living bread. Through his own flesh, now made living and life-giving by the Holy Spirit, he offers life to men."[9] This life is eternal Life, the life of Heaven. Fr. Bernard Blankenhorn, O.P., in his book *Bread from Heaven: An Introduction to The Theology of the Eucharist*, comments: "When we eat and drink the body and blood of the glorified Christ, he renders us immortal, as he conforms us to himself, body and soul. Communion with him also brings us ever closer to the heavenly liturgy, that perpetual worship of the saints before the ascended Lord, the celestial ritual in which every mass on earth already participates."[10]

We join in the celestial worship above because Jesus has made this possible through sharing in His life. In Jesus' own words: "He who eats my flesh and drinks my blood abides in me, and I in him" (John 6:56). St. Augustine, the fourth-century North African bishop and theologian, says that eating the Eucharistic Jesus is not like any other kind of eating. When we eat food, it becomes

---

[8]   Marie Vincent Bernadot, O.P., *The Eucharist and the Trinity* (Michael Glazier, 1977), 19.

[9]   *Ecclesia de Eucharistia*, no. 1, quoting Vatican II, Decree on the Ministry and Life of Priests *Presbyterorum Ordinis*, no. 5.

[10]   Bernhard Blankenhorn, *Bread from Heaven: An Introduction to the Theology of the Eucharist* (Catholic University of America Press, 2021), 2.

part of us. On the natural biological level it is already amazing how food is turned by the body into flesh and blood. However, St. Augustine says that when we chew on the risen, glorious flesh of Christ, we become part of Him, such is the incredible union brought about by receiving the Body of the Lord.

St. Cyril of Jerusalem has a wonderful analogy that captures this reception in its most profound meaning. He says, "Throw melted wax into melted wax, and the one interpenetrates the other perfectly. In the same way, when the body and blood of Christ are received, the union is such that Christ is in the recipient and he in Christ.... We have the same body, and the same blood."[11]

Pope Benedict XVI echoed this teaching in his address at World Youth Day in Cologne. The pope said: "The Body and Blood of Christ are given to us so that we ourselves will be transformed in our turn. We are to become the Body of Christ, his own Flesh and Blood. We all eat the one bread, and this means that we ourselves become one. In this way, adoration, as we said earlier, becomes union. God no longer simply stands before us as the One who is totally Other. He is within us, and we are in him."[12]

This union of being in Christ means that without losing our distinct personalities, we mysteriously become truly one with Christ before our Heavenly Father. The Father can truly look upon us in these moments and see us in His Son in the most intense way. The union is so real that many saints have often said the angels "envy" us because they cannot even tell the difference

---

[11] Quoted in Bernadot, *The Eucharist and the Trinity*, 17.

[12] Pope Benedict XVI, World Youth Day Homily at Holy Mass in the Marienfeld, Cologne, August 21, 2005.

between us and Christ in Holy Communion. Fr. Bernadot captures this amazing mystery of union in striking terms:

> Around the moment we receive Communion, Jesus fills our hearts and our souls so completely that our thoughts and feelings may be said to be His as well.... Together we adore, love and give thanks. Together, we give ourselves to our Father in Heaven. His love and ours, His thoughts and ours, intermingle. Like two grains of incense burned together in the same thurible, they emit one single fragrance towards heaven.[13]

The image here of a single wisp of incense rising is so provocative of the radical miracle of unity that takes place between us and the Lord through the Eucharist: We become more deeply "one mystical person" in Christ.

Before we end today's reflection it is important to highlight that this incredible union wrought by eating the Eucharistic Jesus is not only a moment of intimacy and union. It is an intimate union which brings an *increasing* transformative effusion of life and grace. When we frequently receive Holy Communion, our abiding in Jesus *grows* and we are drawn ever more deeply into the Father's heart. We are drawn there by the power of the Holy Spirit through His Son receiving an increasing inflow of His love, light, and life. We become more divinized as we participate ever more in the divine nature by grace. Put in other words, frequent partaking in the Eucharist effects in us a greater possession of our souls by the Lord. When Jesus possesses us more and more, we receive more of our eternal inheritance. As we read in the *Catechism*: "What material food produces in our bodily

---

[13] Bernadot, *The Eucharist and the Trinity*, 17.

life, Holy Communion wonderfully achieves in our spiritual life. Communion with the flesh of the risen Christ … *preserves, increases, and renews* the life of grace received at Baptism" (no. 1392, emphasis added).

*Let Us Pray:* Lord, give me a deep revelation and understanding of the effects of Your Eucharistic heart upon my life. Help me to hunger for an ever-deeper union with You. Transform my life as a living icon of You.

## Today's Reflection

*Was there a particular thought or line
that spoke to you in this chapter?*

*In this reflection, Fr. Jesse quotes from a number of great
theologians to describe our union with the Eucharistic presence
of Christ. Which spoke most eloquently to your heart?*

*"Holy Communion … is a person-to-person encounter of love."
Have you experienced this? If not, ask God for this grace.*

*Did you know that the principal fruit of the Eucharist
is to transform you into Christ? Have you given much
thought to the effects of the Eucharist in your life?*

Day 4

# Bride from the
# Side of Christ

*Because there is one bread, we who are many are
one body, for we all partake of the one bread.*

—1 Corinthians 10:17

Eve came forth from the rib of Adam. Adam then became a bridegroom. The Church, the Bride of Christ, comes forth from her Bridegroom's side that was pierced upon the Cross. This has been the traditional understanding of the symbol of the blood and water streaming from the pierced side of Christ. The blood and water symbolize the sacraments. The sacraments are Christ's chosen instruments by which He brings His Bride into existence. It is the means by which He communicates Himself to us. Through the sacraments, this Divine Bridegroom breathes His very own life into His spouse the Church, making her one with Him.

The sacraments constitute also the saving activity of grace breaking into the world through the Church. The activity of the Church is the activity of Christ, who wants to bring all things into Himself. He created the Church to bring His creation back into full communion with His Father. The most important means by which Christ does this is the sacrament of the Eucharist. The Eucharist is the most important sacrament because it is the Lord Himself. He is the entire treasury of all the graces that makes the Church. The Eucharist, therefore, is the source and summit of the Church's life.

The Church's life is the life of Christ. This is why St. Paul teaches us that the nature of this life is something mystical, something supernatural, something divine. The Church is not a series of buildings. She is what St. Paul calls the Mystical Body of Christ. This body is structured hierarchically and takes the form of a global society, but nevertheless, it is more than that: It is a living organism, a whole new creation brought into existence by Christ after His death and Resurrection. This new creation is a work of grace, a work of the Holy Spirit.

We must stretch our minds to think with faith when we think of the true nature of the Church. Her nature will not be revealed to us by reason alone. It calls for the awe and wonder of faith-knowledge. Too often, people have a very limited understanding of the Church, as if she is only an institution or a religious body of rules. The truth of who she is, is truly incredible: Christ has created her to be His very body and presence on earth. While the ascended Christ is in Heaven, Christ lives in her, thinks through her, acts on earth through her. He created her to be one with Him. This is why He calls her His Bride. Of course, when we speak of the Church, we speak of all those Christians who have been baptized into this new creation of Christ' body. We are all the Church, since we are all members of Christ. We live in His Mystical Body. We must really let this truth sink into our hearts. It changes the way we see each other.

Yesterday we saw how Holy Communion transforms us in Christ. Today we meditate on how this also has an effect on our unity with other members in the Church. The Eucharist strengthens our bond as brothers and sisters in Christ. The *Catechism* instructs:

> Those who receive the Eucharist are united more closely to Christ. Through it Christ unites them to all the faithful in one body—the Church. Communion renews, strengthens, and deepens this incorporation into the Church, already achieved by Baptism. In Baptism we have been called to form but one body. The Eucharist fulfills this call: "The cup of blessing which we bless, is it not a participation in the blood of Christ? The bread which we break, is it not a participation in the body of Christ? Because there is one bread, we who are many are one body, for we all partake of the one bread." (no. 1396)

St. John Chrysostom reflects on this reality in a compelling manner:

> For what is the bread? It is the body of Christ. And what do those who receive it become? The Body of Christ—not many bodies but one body. For as bread is completely one, though made of up many grains of wheat, and these, albeit unseen, remain nonetheless present, in such a way that their difference is not apparent since they have been made a perfect whole, so too are we mutually joined to one another and together united with Christ.[14]

These words reinforce the work of unity that the celebration and reception of the Eucharist bring about.

---

[14] St. John Chrysostom, "Homily 24, 1 Corinthians 10:16," *Homilies on First Corinthians*, trans. Talbot W. Chambers, in *Nicene and Post-Nicene Fathers*, 1st series, vol. 12, ed. Philip Shaff (Buffalo, NY, 1889), https://www.newadvent.org/fathers/2201.htm.

In a similar vein, in his encyclical letter *Ecclesia de Eucharistia*, St. John Paul II speaks of how the Eucharistic celebration of Holy Mass leads to the Church's supernatural development in the life of grace. Have you ever thought of that? The more the Holy Mass is celebrated, the greater the spiritual growth of the Church. The great pope of the Eucharist writes:

> The Second Vatican Council teaches that the celebration of the Eucharist is at the centre of the process of the Church's growth.... [A]s if in answer to the question: "How does the Church grow?", the Council adds: "as often as the sacrifice of the Cross by which 'Christ our pasch is sacrificed' (*1 Cor* 5:7) is celebrated on the altar, the work of our redemption is carried out. At the same time in the sacrament of the Eucharistic bread, the unity of the faithful, who form one body in Christ (cf. *1 Cor* 10:17), is both expressed and brought about."[15]

It is truly a magnificent thought to think of the Church and the Mass in these terms. It highlights the supernatural nature of the Church and how powerfully life-giving is the celebration of the Eucharist in Holy Mass. This truth ought to help elevate our minds to the beauty of the Holy Mass. It is like the heartbeat that pumps out the love of God into the Church and through her into the world. St. Padre Pio said that the earth can last longer without the sun than it can without the celebration of the Holy Mass. He obviously deeply grasped the incredible impact of the Holy Mass on the world. Maybe we need to capture this outlook of seeing the indispensability of the Holy Mass and the Eucharist. This calls for the eyes of faith.

---

[15] *Ecclesia de Eucharistia*, no. 21.

Reflect on the truth that the Eucharist makes the Church. Christ the divine Bridegroom celebrates the Holy Mass through the priest in order to give us His body so that we can all become what we eat. We become one. We become brothers and sisters in the Lord. Next time you go to Communion, try to be aware of how you are being bonded more deeply with all your brothers and sisters in Christ. Note how the Church is not just a society or institution but a Mystical Body of believers who are united to Jesus in spirit.

*Let Us Pray:* Lord, may I thirst for a deeper bond to all those You have called to Yourself. May I love my fellow Christians as I love myself, seeing that they are one with me in You. Lord, call many priests to your vineyard, so that the celebration of the Holy Mass may contribute to the Church's growth.

## Today's Reflection

*What would you say if someone asked
you, "What is the Church?"*

*How do you experience the unity of the Body of Christ?*

*Did you ever think of the celebration of Mass
as giving spiritual growth to the Church?*

*Do you think today's teaching has transformed
your perspective of the Holy Mass?*

Day 5

# Sent with Love

*I know I would not be able to work one week*
*if it were not for that continual force coming*
*from Jesus in the Blessed Sacrament.*

—St. Teresa of Calcutta (Mother Teresa)

As we have seen, the Eucharist involves a series of transformations that culminate in the soul being more intimately transformed in Christ. Yesterday we saw how this transformation also binds us together into the reality of the Church. There is another fruit of the Eucharist worth pondering: the transformation of the soul in love to be sent to love.

One of the greatest deeds of Christ in the Eucharist is to ignite and increase his love in and through us. To have contact with the Eucharistic Lord is to have contact with the very vitalizing source of love and life that enables the Church's mission. This is not fiction; it is a reality.

The Church is the chosen bearer of Christ's love to the world. Our Christian Faith is not a private faith. We belong to a community—one with a mission of sanctifying the world with the love of God. The Eucharist is the Bread of Life for our journey to Heaven. It energizes and assists us to live the commandments of Jesus, especially the command to love. Love is the hallmark of the Christian life. If Christianity has a brand name, it is love. This truth is rooted in Jesus' command to us: "A new commandment I give to you, that you love one another; even as I have loved you, that you also love one another. By this all men will know that you are my disciples, if you have love for one another" (John 13:34–35).

St. Catherine of Siena received a very powerful revelation from God the Father about the reason why we are commanded to love our neighbor. The Father explains to Catherine that in loving our neighbor we get to love in the way God loves us. God the Father says to her:

> I ask you to love me with the same love with which I love you. But for me you cannot do this, for I loved you without being loved. Whatever love you have for me you owe me, so you love me not gratuitously but out of duty, while I love you not out of duty but gratuitously. So you cannot give the kind of love I ask of you. This is why I have put you among your neighbors: so that you can do for them what you cannot do for me—that is, love them without any concern for thanks and without looking for any profit for yourself. And whatever you do for them I will consider done for me.[16]

If the Father asks us to freely love our neighbor in the way He loves us, He will give us the grace to do it. As the old saying goes, Jesus always gives grace for things He asks of us. The Lord furnishes us with every grace to carry out our mission of love.

---

[16] St. Catherine of Siena, *The Dialogue*, trans. Susan Noffke, O.P. (Paulist Press, 1980), 121.

When Jesus comes to us in Holy Communion, Love Himself comes. He comes with the power to renew in us our ability to love. The *Catechism* instructs us: "As bodily nourishment restores lost strength, so the Eucharist strengthens our charity, which tends to be weakened in daily life.... By giving himself to us, Christ revives our love" (no. 1394). This renewed love is meant for us to transform the world with love. Pope Benedict XVI, addressing the World Youth Day gathering in Cologne, highlighted this movement of love: "His dynamic enters into us and then seeks to spread outwards to others until it fills the world, so that his love can truly become the dominant measure of the world."[17]

St. Mother Teresa of Calcutta was convicted of this dynamic effect of the Eucharist. She attributed all her charity missions and the source of her love to the Eucharistic Lord coming to her in Holy Mass and Eucharistic Adoration. Mother never compromised her prayer of Eucharistic Adoration. She encouraged her sisters to do the same. She emphasized to them that without the Eucharist they would have no love to give. Mother once said it like this: "I know I would not be able to work one week if it were not for that continual force coming from Jesus in the Blessed Sacrament."[18] Similarly, St. John Paul II often expressed that he was only able to accomplish his demanding work because of sharing in the Eucharistic banquet and his habit of long prayer before the tabernacle.

I have been in the habit of asking people their lived ordinary experience of the Eucharist; their response always points to the

---

[17] Pope Benedict XVI, World Youth Day homily in Marienfeld, August 21, 2005.

[18] Quoted in "The Spirituality of Bl. Mother Teresa of Calcutta, in Her Own Words," Missionaries of the Blessed Sacrament, http://acfp2000.com/Saints-Mother-Teresa.html.

Eucharist as a source of immense renewal. One young altar server recently told me that he experienced great strength from Holy Communion. How beautiful to hear these effects of the Eucharist, which flow from the love of God. Receiving Jesus with an open heart restores peace, helps us forgive, and aids us in our commitment to love those we find difficult. Our lives would look a lot different if we were not filled up with the graces from the Eucharist. This effect of love is not something we should take for granted. We should prepare well for Holy Communion if we are to receive the full effects of our Eucharistic Lord.

*Let Us Pray:* Lord, I beg of You every grace of love the next time I receive You into my life. Burn my heart with love and mercy for my neighbors. Strengthen me with a firm will and heart overflowing with the resolve to do good for others.

## Today's Reflection

*Was there a particular line in this reflection that was especially meaningful to you?*

*"How beautiful to hear these effects of the Eucharist, which flow from the love of God." What did this make you think of? What effects have you experienced from the Eucharist?*

*Do you see the Eucharist as the source from which you can grow in love?*

Day 6

# The Eucharist and the Poor

*You have tasted the Blood of the Lord, yet
you do not recognize your brother.*

—St. John Chrysostom

As Christians, we ought to love who and what Jesus loves. When we are really united to Jesus, He lives His life in us and we start to think His thoughts and do His actions. He prompts us to act and think in these ways by the Holy Spirit. One of the signs of a deep union with Jesus is concern and compassion for the afflicted and poor. St. John Paul II often preached that the Church has a preferential option for the poor because Christ had this preferential option. The Church must love what Jesus loves because she is His Mystical Body on earth. She has His heart. As we have seen, Jesus lives in her in a mysterious way.

Archbishop Jason Gordon once told me that the Church has three main treasures: the Eucharist, Our Blessed Mother Mary, and the poor. Another missionary I know said that the Lord spoke to her heart in prayer that she knew nothing about His Kingdom unless she went and sat with the poor. People who have little but have faith can show us what it means to really depend on the Lord for everything. This is why some of the greatest graces of prayer and divine signs are given to the poor. They are in touch with a deep hunger for grace and Jesus' love. I have seen this in my own short and limited experience as a priest. The less fortunate have a lot to teach the wealthier parts of the Church, including the clergy.

One of the fruits of the Eucharist, whether it is from Holy Communion or from adoring Jesus in the tabernacle or monstrance, is to develop a sensitive love for the poor. The *Catechism* identifies this as a specific fruit of the Eucharist: "*The Eucharist commits us to the poor. To receive in truth the Body and Blood of Christ given up for us, we must recognize Christ in the poorest, his brethren.*" (no. 1397).

In the same paragraph, we find a challenging word from St. John Chrysostom:

> You have tasted the Blood of the Lord, yet you do not recognize your brother.... You dishonor this table when you do not judge worthy of sharing your food someone judged worthy to take part in this meal.... God freed you from all your sins and invited you here, but you have not become more merciful.

The saints recognized the great relationship between Christ and the suffering of others. Many of them received the grace to contemplate the face of Christ in the poor and the poorest of the poor. Two saints come to mind: St. Mother Teresa of Calcutta and St. Charles de Foucauld. Both Mother and St. Charles saw a deep connection between the Eucharistic Jesus and the poor. Both understood that adoration of the Eucharist is meant to overflow in good works toward the poor.

Mother describes her conviction: "The Holy Hour before the Eucharist must lead us to the holy hour with the poor, with those who will never have human accomplishments and for whom the sole consolations will be Jesus. Our Eucharist is incomplete if it does not lead us to the service and love of the poor."[19]

For Mother it was the habit of adoration that allowed her to discover Jesus in the distressing disguise of the poor. Mother is famous for having said: "All of us know that unless we believe and can see Jesus in the appearance of bread on the altar, we will not be able to see him in the distressing disguise of the poor." Mother's point is simple: If we develop the habit of contemplating the face of Christ in the Eucharist, we will have a greater disposition and ability to contemplate His face in the poor. Adoration leads to an increased sensitivity of seeing Christ in the needs of others. The Eucharist appears as bread to our senses, but by faith we see Jesus. Similarly, the suffering of the poor appears just as it does in other people, but faith tells us Jesus is present before us in them and their affliction. Mother had a firm foundation for this belief because of the words of Jesus:

> "For I was hungry and you gave me no food, I was thirsty and you gave me no drink, I was a stranger and you did not welcome me, naked and you did not clothe me, sick and in prison and you did not visit me." Then they also will answer, "Lord, when did we see thee hungry or thirsty or a stranger or naked or sick or in prison, and did not minister to thee?" Then he will answer them, "Truly, I say

---

[19] Blessed Mother Teresa, *Tu m'apportes l'amour*, Écrits spirituels (Éditions du Centurion, 1975).

to you, as you did it not to one of the least of these, you did it not to me." (Matt. 25:42–45).

St. Charles de Foucauld, whose life and love of the Eucharist we will explore more deeply later in this book, always tried to bring the Eucharist close to the poor. He could see the poverty of Jesus Himself in the Eucharist: The Lord of all Glory humbling Himself to come to us under the appearance of bread is a sign of this poverty. I have no doubt that St. Charles's love for the poor stemmed from his many hours of adoration of the Eucharistic Jesus in his hermitage in the Sahara Desert. In the deep silence of prayer, he learned that he was to bring Jesus in the Blessed Sacrament to the most forsaken places. St. Charles had a conviction that Jesus would radiate His love on the poorest of the poor in the Sahara. He believed with a deep intuition that by simply adoring Jesus in the Eucharist in the midst of the Tuareg people of Algeria, many great graces would flow to the community he served. It was in their faces that he saw the same Jesus with whom he was alone in his tabernacle in his hermitage.

*Let Us Pray:* Blessed be Jesus in the poorest of the poor! Lord, give me eyes of faith to see You in the poor. Help me to be in the habit of contemplating Your face in the suffering of others. May my time in adoration of your Eucharistic face help me grow in this sensitivity. Jesus, give me the graces in Holy Communion that help me grow in love for the least fortunate in my life.

## Today's Reflection

*Where do you encounter "the poor" in your life?*
*Poverty takes many forms, not all directly related*
*to money. What is their greatest need, and how*
*is God asking you to respond to that need?*

*Is there someone in your life that you neglect?*

*Do you try to look beyond the appearance*
*of your neighbor to find Christ?*

# A Shield Against Sin

*The more we share the life of Christ and
progress in his friendship, the more difficult it is
to break away from him by mortal sin.*

—*Catechism of the Catholic Church*, no. 1395

By now, you can see that the Eucharistic Jesus brings about many fruits in His communion with us. We have been pondering how the Bread of Life actually has an impact on our lives. To receive the Eucharistic Jesus is not only a holy thing to do, it makes us holy, it changes us. There are still more fruits and effects of the Eucharistic Jesus to ponder and hold in our hearts. Understanding them will help increase our desire for Holy Communion.

Here is a question: Do you desire holiness? Holiness is our union with the life of grace; that is, the life of Christ Himself. Holiness means our divinization in Christ, which brings us to share in the triune love of God. It means becoming an heir with Christ to every grace and blessing poured out in the Holy Spirit by God the Father. It means having the mind of Christ whereby Christ is alive in our thoughts, thinking through us. It means that Jesus is so alive in us that our actions become His actions. Holiness is a union of hearts between Jesus' heart and our own. Our Blessed Mother Mary is a perfect model of human holiness because her heart was completely in unison with that of her Son. The mystery of her sinless life is the foundation of this complete union. Therefore, the greatest enemy to holiness is sin.

Sin separates us from the divine life of Jesus. It makes us act and think in ways infinitely incompatible with the life of the Most Holy Trinity. It distorts our minds and hearts in a way that makes us lose the mind of Christ. When we sin, our union with the triune life of God is eaten away. This is why when we attend Holy Mass we confess even venial sins[20] at the beginning, to permit us to enter deeply into the heart of Christ. The priest says, "Let us acknowledge our sins so to prepare ourselves to celebrate the sacred mysteries." We prepare ourselves by confessing in order to receive the purifying action of Christ whereby we are cleansed of sin and united more deeply with Him.

When we receive the Lord and consume Him in Holy Communion, He not only comes with grace to renew us in Himself, He also distances us from sin. To use the language of the *Catechism*, "*Holy Communion separates us from sin....* [T]he Eucharist cannot unite us to Christ without at the same time cleansing us from past sins and preserving us from future sins" (no. 1393). The *Catechism* goes on to say that the Eucharist not only protects us from venial sin but also "*preserves us from future mortal sins.*" It says that the "more we share the life of Christ and progress in

---

[20] Venial sins are those sins which affect our union with Christ but do not sever it completely. For a sin to be mortal, the act must be gravely sinful, done freely without any coercion, and done with knowledge of the severity of the sin (see CCC, no. 1859).

his friendship, the more difficult it is to break away from him by mortal sin" (no.1395).

Mortal sin severs our union with God to the point that we lose the life of Christ in our hearts. If we persist in it, and die in such a state, we can also lose our eternal inheritance, our salvation. The loss of salvation is a sobering thought, but it is a real possibility, and we should never underestimate the influence sin has on our hearts and minds to pull us away from the Lord, even to the point of being eternally separated from His love.

The ordinary way to restore our souls to union with God after mortal sin is the sacrament of Confession. Jesus instituted and entrusted this sacrament to His priests as a means of ministering His infinite mercy. Confession of all mortal sin is necessary before we can consume the Eucharist. It is gravely disordered to consume the Eucharist while conscious of grave sin; it is to eat death. We should never presume we can do whatever we want and that we will be saved. Sin is messy and dangerous. It can make us so disfigured that we get stuck in choosing a path away from Christ. It hardens our hearts against the voice of God. It makes us lose the taste for prayer and for good works by destroying love in our hearts.[21]

It is only when we recognize the real danger of losing our eternal life that we can truly appreciate what an enormous gift the Eucharistic Lord is to us in protecting us from such a danger by shielding us from sin and keeping divine love alive in us. The good news is that the only place for sin is under the feet of Christ, who is victorious over sin. Our hope is so great because Christ shares His power over sin with us. He destroys sin in

---

[21] On the other hand, St. Thomas tells us that any act of charity cleanses the heart of venial sin, because charity is the life of God.

us through the sacrament of Confession and shields us from it in the Eucharist. When we receive Him in the Eucharist, we receive an abundant supply of grace to help us overcome our sinful ways.

St. Bernard of Clairvaux says, "If we do not experience so frequent and violent attacks of anger, envy and concupiscence as formerly, let us give thanks to Jesus Christ in the Blessed Sacrament, who has produced these effects in us."[22] Many saints like St. Bernard counsel people to frequent Communion in order to overcome addictions and habitual sin. The proof is in the lived experience of so many who have found so many moral victories because of the infusion divine assistance has given to them through the Eucharistic heart of Christ. As a priest, I have met countless people who have told me about the strength and power they receive through frequent Communion and especially from much time in Eucharistic Adoration.

Before we end our reflection today, I would like to spell out some more of the graces that Holy Communion communicates to our souls. As we have been saying, the Eucharistic Jesus offers us graces to help preserve and strengthen us against sin. Here is a question: What do we mean by these "graces"?

Fr. James Brent, O.P., can help us define these graces. The way he breaks down the term *grace* clarifies how the Eucharist helps us against sin. Writing about graces, Fr. James says:

The most fundamental one is *sanctifying grace*. For now, let us just say that sanctifying grace is something of God's own *life* planted in the depths of our souls.... Flowing

---

[22] Quoted in Michael Mueller, C.S.S.R., *The Blessed Eucharist: Our Greatest Treasure* (TAN Books, 1868), 102.

from sanctifying grace are all the *infused virtues* as well as the *gifts and fruits of the Holy Spirit.* According to the traditional list, the infused virtues are faith, hope, love, prudence, justice, temperance, and fortitude. The gifts of the Spirit are understanding, knowledge, wisdom, counsel, piety, fortitude, and fear of the Lord. The fruits of the Spirit are love, joy, peace, patience, kindness, goodness, generosity, gentleness, faithfulness, modesty, self-control, and chastity.

He goes on to say that "sanctifying grace, the virtues, gifts, and fruits" are aids by God to "form the very capacity to welcome God personally and respond to him consciously and freely on a level beyond all that is possible for us to do by our own human strength or abilities."[23] This response to God is the life-long Christian journey. In other words, when God is shielding us from sin through these graces in the Eucharist, He is really enabling us to respond more and more to the gift of Himself in our lives. He is fortifying us to become His more and more.

*Let Us Pray:* Lord, strengthen in me my ability to choose Your way of life. Help me be convinced that your Eucharistic heart will bring me an abundance of life. Protect me from my sins that empty me of Your presence and peace. Revive in me a strong determination to overcome my addictions and weaknesses. Turn everything for Your greater glory and my growth in holiness. Let me regret nothing because of Your merciful love.

---

[23] Fr. James Brent, O.P., "The Graces of God," *Spiritual Direction,* August 16, 2022, https://spiritualdirection.com/2022/08/16 /the-graces-of-god.

## Today's Reflection

*Is there a particular sin that has a "grip" on your soul?
Do not be embarrassed to bring it to Confession. Jesus
wants to free you from your burden. Ask the Lord to
shower you with the graces you need to overcome.*

*Have you experienced the strength of the Eucharist against sin?*

*How would you describe sanctifying grace to someone?*

Day 8

# Dispositions of Heart

*Some one touched me; for I perceive that*
*power has gone forth from me.*

–Luke 8:46

Yesterday we saw how the Bread of Life truly protects us from
sinning by strengthening our will against sin. Over the last few
days, we have seen how receiving Holy Communion can actually
change our lives in mystical and also practical ways. Today we need
to meditate on how the effects of Holy Communion with Jesus
depend on the disposition of our hearts.

When Jesus comes with all His power and grace to make us His
own by transforming us into Himself, the extent of this transformation depends on our preparation and openness of heart. Our
hearts are shaped above all by our faith, hope, and love. These
are the most fundamental divine graces, which help us produce
acts of the soul that bring us to union with the source of all life,
God. I often think of these three virtues like the three prongs of
a plug that are placed in the "divine electricity socket" of grace.
When we approach the altar, our faith, hope, and love draw power

from the Eucharistic heart of Jesus. The greater these virtues in our soul, the greater our capacity to receive the unimaginable light and life that Jesus Christ is communicating to us in Holy Communion and in Eucharistic Adoration.

Throughout the Gospels, we see again and again the primacy of faith that touches the heart of Jesus and ends in Jesus moving immediately to act with power and healing. We can speak of the primacy of faith because our hope and love draw power from the degree of our faith. What exactly is faith? Faith is a grace that allows us to have a real living contact with God. It is not just trust and belief; it is a grace given to us by which God draws us to acknowledge with our hearts and minds that He is true and real. In essence, by infusing faith into a soul, the Lord reveals Himself in the innermost sanctuary of the heart and mind as Truth. God becomes truly present in the soul, effecting an infusion of light. This is why we could say faith brings about a real contact with God. Bl. Columba Marmion once said that because of this contact, when we think of Jesus, it is not only a holy thing to do: Thinking of Him in faith makes us touch Him, and in touching Him we are sanctified and made to grow in holiness. That would make you want to think of Jesus often!

When we approach Holy Communion with a lively faith, our contact with Jesus deepens and all the effects we have spoken about the last few days grow more and more in us. The same is true of Eucharistic Adoration, which is a form of spiritual communion with Jesus. When we go to Eucharistic Adoration, faith brings us deep into His heart truly alive in the tabernacle or monstrance. Faith makes us have a real touch on Jesus in adoration. Touching Him, faith draws power from Him beyond our wildest imaginations. In his book *Fire & Light*, Fr. Jacques Philippe, a modern day master of the spiritual life, says that "through love of the Eucharist, we discover that an act of faith opens us to unexpected realities, which, although mysterious and puzzling to our human faculties, are no less solidly real, true reference points for our interior transformation and human and spiritual growth."[24] He also says that "the hours spent in silent meditation before the Blessed Sacrament all are certain finally to bring us to a true experience of God in which we see clearly we are approaching the ultimate reality. Sometimes, paradoxically, this mystery so poor and confusing in appearances gives us moments of fullness and happiness surpassing anything earth can bestow."[25] Brothers and sisters, this is the fruit of persevering in faith and prayer before the mystery of our Eucharistic Jesus.

What about hope? St. John of the Cross says: "The soul obtains from God as much as it hopes from him." Hope is crucial for the spiritual life. Sometimes we forget that we are also saved by hoping in God. We cannot be saved if we do not hope in the Lord. Christian hope yearns for eternal life and happiness with God in eternity. Our hope is anchored on the divine assistance the good Lord promised to give us to bring us to Heaven. Christian hope is also nourished in a paradoxical way by our poverty and weakness. When we know we are weak and incapable of the heights of holiness by ourselves, we can only lean on the Lord, we can only hope in God who "is able to provide you with every blessing in abundance, so that you may always have enough of everything and may provide in abundance for every good work" (2 Cor. 9:8). Our weakness refines our faith and hope because it causes us to make a greater act of faith and hope in God's loving goodness when we are faced with our failures. Fr. Philippe captures

---

[24] Philippe, *Fire and Light*, 98.
[25] Ibid., 97.

so well how our weakness draws us to God: "The experience of radical weakness compels us to a kind of surrender by which we recognize our poverty, accept the fact that we are not absolute masters of our lives, count on God alone, and place ourselves at his mercy with boundless trust. Then God acts and does splendid things, things sometimes visible but often hidden."[26] When we come with hope before the Eucharistic Lord, great things happen in our souls and in the world! He is attracted by our hope.

Both faith and hope lead to the crown of the spiritual life, love. Our desire and love for Jesus flourish when we have a deep faith and hope. It is also true that our love of God gives us an experiential knowledge of Him which strengthens faith and hope. What faith tells us is real, hope drives us to obtain, and love experiences and obtains. Love is possession and union with God. The saints tell us that the greater our love for Jesus, the greater our union with Him and the greater the torrent of grace flowing from His heart. There is no grace Jesus does not want to give, because there is no grace Jesus did not die to give. It is in this light that St. Thomas Aquinas calls the Eucharist the sacrament of divine love; through the Eucharist, Jesus gives without counting the cost, He gives without limit, He gives Himself completely. It is why the Eucharist is a memorial of the Lord's Passion: It enshrines His ultimate love given on the Cross. Jesus gave us the meaning of the Cross when He said, "Greater love has no man than this, that a man lay down his life for his friends" (John 15:13). In other words, there is no boundary to what the Lord wants to give us through the Eucharist. It is us who place the limit.

We overcome the limit by love. It is love in us which opens the deepest recesses of our being to desire to receive the love of

---

[26] Ibid., 45.

Jesus. I think this is what St. Mother Teresa meant when she said "Holiness is an excess of love." When one grows in love, it attracts even more love. The more we love the heart of Jesus, the more He will give us Himself in love. Our ability to experience the love of Jesus in Holy Communion and in Eucharistic Adoration depends on the extent we too are willing to lay down our life in love for the Lord. This is a fundamental spiritual law.

Therefore, if we approach Jesus with a heart open with faith, hope, and love, we shall expect to grow from grace to grace. If we are little affected in our lives from the Bread of Life, it is because these virtues are weak in our souls and we have placed obstacles to them. Thankfully we can turn to God and say, "Lord, I believe. Help my unbelief!" The same is true of hope and love.

*Let Us Pray:* Lord please give me the right dispositions of heart that help me draw forth the greatest effect of your Eucharistic heart. Help my faith, hope, and love.

## Today's Reflection

*Do you find it hard to find Jesus hidden in the Eucharist?*

*Do you pray for the virtue of hope, or do you focus on asking God for faith and love?*

*Have you been grateful for your weakness as a source of your hope?*

Day 9

# Living the Word

*He who has my commandments and keeps them, he it is
who loves me; and he who loves me will be loved by my
Father, and I will love him and manifest myself to him.*

—John 14:21

Yesterday we spoke about the importance of the prayer of faith,
hope and love in our receptivity of the grace of the Holy Eucharist.
Today we want to muse on how these virtues are strengthened.

It is a rule of the spiritual life that virtues can grow in the
soul. This is true for faith, hope, and love. The more we make
acts of faith, hope, and love, the more we grow in these virtues
as they take a deeper root in our hearts. However, these virtues
are directly affected by our life and moral choices. Sin eats away at
these virtues in our soul and so it directly impacts on our union
with Christ, which hinges principally on these three virtues.

How we live each day of our lives—not only at Mass, but every
moment—is significant. How often, and how earnestly, we turn
to God in prayer throughout the week determines how open
our hearts are to the graces God wants to give us during Holy

Communion. Ordinarily, we cannot expect to receive great graces from Jesus in Holy Communion if we spend the rest of our lives distant from Him. Our hearts are shaped by our moral actions. We become what we say and do. In order to really reap the powerful graces of Holy Communion, we must have a sincere commitment to live the gospel and keep free from sin as much as possible. If we are to discover the living presence of Jesus in the Eucharist and have Him manifest Himself to us in Eucharistic Adoration or Holy Communion, we must heed His own words: "He who has my commandments and keeps them, he it is who loves me; and he who loves me will be loved by my Father, and I will love him and *manifest myself to him*" (John 14:21, emphasis added).

Following Jesus' gospel is a fundamental means to our prayerful experience of Christ and to Him revealing Himself more to us. We cannot labor this point too much. If we refuse His word—that is, if we continue to act in ways contrary to His word through sin—we can't expect to come to truly know or experience the Lord. Our love for the Lord will be affected, and it is love which draws all graces. Hence, attachments to sin militate against a life of divine grace in the soul. They are barriers to our Eucharistic Lord.

St. Thomas Aquinas teaches that venial sin impairs the effects of the Eucharistic Jesus. He quotes St. John Damascene as saying: "The fire of that desire which is within us, being kindled by the burning coal" of the Eucharist "will consume our sins, and enlighten our hearts, so that we shall be inflamed and made godlike." However, St. Thomas goes on to say: "But the fire of our desire or love is hindered by venial sins, which hinder the fervor of charity."[27] The point is our venial sins act as a barrier between us and Christ. Despite this, however, St. Thomas does

---

[27] St. Thomas Aquinas, *Summa Theologiae* III, q. 79, art. 8.

not leave us without hope, since he also says, "It can come to pass that after many venial sins a man may approach devoutly to this sacrament and fully secure its effect."[28] In other words, even if one has sinned venially, if one finds repentance and a firm devotion to not be attached to sin, one can receive the effects of the sacrament.

As already mentioned, the surest way to benefit from the Eucharist is the gospel way of life. Following the gospel is unlike following any other religious or human wisdom. It is to follow the true path of life revealed by God Himself in Christ Jesus. No other person in history can boast of this path to Heaven. No one else in history can bring us to eternal life. Jesus said, "I am the way, and the truth, and the life" (John 14:6). Jesus isn't just any person, He is God. He made us to be His forever. He knows how to do this. We can trust His testimony and His words. When we live the gospel path set forth by Christ, it actually transforms our being in its deepest core. We not only become more like Christ in our actions; Christ actually lives His life in us more deeply.

Let's return to the main point of today's reflection: Living the Word of God is the best preparation for receiving the transformative effects of our Eucharistic Jesus. If I do not adhere to God's Word, this is already a lack of faith, hope, and love in God. I am convinced that if we find ourselves as both hearers and doers of the Word as transmitted in the Scriptures and the living tradition of the Church, we will find a greater ability to receive the same Word of God coming to us in sacramental form in the Eucharist. If we are accustomed to receiving Jesus in the way He comes into our hearts through living His commandments and His words of life, our hearts will already have an affinity to Jesus

---

[28] Ibid.

in His Eucharistic Body and Blood. If we ask ourselves why so many are unaffected by Holy Communion, we will understand the answer to be directly proportionate to how much people conform their lives in faith to Jesus' Word. The point is clear: The more obedient we are to the Word of God, the greater the capacity of our hearts to receive all the supernatural life stored up in Jesus' Eucharistic heart.

*Let Us Pray:* Lord, give me a docile heart to hear Your word and to live it with all my strength. Remove in me any sin or disordered attachment that prevents me from receiving fully all Your gracious effects in the Most Holy Eucharist.

## Today's Reflection

*Did you ever see a connection between your growth
in prayer and the moral choices you make?*

*Living the Word of God is the best preparation
for receiving the graces of God. How is God
asking you to live that truth this week?*

*What area of your life is stopping you
from a deeper experience of God?*

Day 10

# Eucharistic Lives

*I appeal to you therefore, brethren, by the mercies of
God, to present your bodies as a living sacrifice, holy and
acceptable to God, which is your spiritual worship.*

—Romans 12:1

Every saint lives a deeply Eucharistic life. They understand life to
be Eucharistic. What does this mean? Essentially, to be Eucharistic
means to be *sacrificial.* Traditionally we understand the Eucharist
as a sacrifice. The Eucharistic supper is a sacrificial meal. There
are four ends to sacrifice: thanksgiving, adoration, supplication,
and expiation (atonement). To be Eucharistic therefore means to
live one's life toward the Lord in thanksgiving, in adoration, in
supplication, and in expiation.

Living a Eucharistic life can also mean offering ourselves as
victims of love to the Lord. It speaks to the way the Lord prepares
us through suffering and trials to be purified for the offering of our
lives as spotless and holy to Him. On this note, our Christian lives
find in the Eucharistic celebration a real blueprint as to how the
Lord prepares us daily for our ultimate goal, transformation in Him.

How is this the case? We can understand something of our own journeys of purification in the journey of the bread and wine to the altar to become Christ. The journey is one of sacrifice. Let us ponder this in light of the preparation of wheat and grapes for the bread and wine to be offered in the Eucharist. In their preparation we see a series of transformations which also echo our own life experience. To prepare for the bread to be offered at Mass, wheat is sifted and gathered and changed into bread. Grapes are crushed and fermented into wine. This is a work of both preparation and purification. On the symbolic level, this speaks to our own lives, which need to be sifted and gathered together in integrity and holiness. We have to be made whole because of the fragmenting effects of sin. As the grapes are crushed and fermented, so we have to be tried by many trials in order to be purified: "Through many tribulations we must enter the kingdom of God" (Acts 14:22). What emerges from the gathering of wheat and the fermenting of grapes is something wholly new.

There is a profound truth in the fact that neither wheat nor grapes can bring themselves to become the something "new" of bread and wine. They depend on the actions of human beings. In a similar way, the preparation of our lives as a work of holiness can only be a work of grace, of the Lord acting on us by His power. It is the Lord who sifts us, who gathers our powers of intellect and will together toward choosing the path of grace; it is the Lord who makes us holy. We cooperate with our freedom, but it is ultimately His free work of grace. It is a very liberating truth to know and believe.

St. Paul says, "It is God who is at work in you, enabling you both to will and to work for his good pleasure" (Phil. 2:13, NRSVCE). Jesus puts it like this: "Apart from me you can do nothing" (John 15:5). To be a Eucharistic people means our transformation can only come from Christ.

The Holy Mass should always remind us of this great truth, since the bread and wine cannot become Christ without Christ's action of grace. The bread and wine are transformed by the powerful words of Jesus speaking and acting through the priest in the Mass. The *Catechism* quotes St. John Chrysostom as declaring: "It is not man that causes the things offered to become the Body and Blood of Christ, but he who was crucified for us, Christ himself. The priest, in the role of Christ, pronounces these words, but their power and grace are God's. This is my body, he says. This word transforms the things offered" (no. 1375).

There is an Irish man named Jim Coney whose grave in Newbridge, Ireland, has an inscription that attests to this mystery: "Whatever Jesus says, *is*." When he says, "This is my body," "This is my blood," it *is*. His words bring about the unthinkable: Creation becomes the Creator, bread and wine become Jesus' very Body and Blood. It becomes Him. Again, we should see this action of Christ speaking His words over the offerings of bread and wine as indicative for His own speaking over our own lives. In a certain sense this should teach us to listen to and receive the Word of God, which has a transformative power to convert our souls and bring them into a deeper union with Christ. When we live according to the gospel, we grow in grace and the life of Jesus deepens in us. We become doers of the Word—our lives become a sort of living scripture.

The journey of grapes and bread ends in Christ. It teaches that even the creation will eventually end in Christ, when the whole world will be transformed at the end of time when Christ comes again in His glory at the Second Coming. It also means our journey as Christians is to end in Christ in Heaven. The saints in Heaven are those who have become fully conformed to Christ. To become Christ is our life's true purpose.

*Let Us Pray:* Lord, help me see the journey of the bread and wine to the altar as the journey of Your own life. Help me accept my trials as the means by which You prepare me to be transformed more into You. Teach me to cultivate an attitude that sees a connection between the Holy Mass and my everyday life.

## Today's Reflection

*The wheat and grapes cannot turn themselves into bread and wine; they must be acted upon. The same is true of us. Where do you sense God is at work in you right now? How is God turning your life into a "living scripture"?*

*Which of the four "ends" of sacrifice do you need to work on? Which one comes easiest to you?*

*Have you made the link between your life and the altar? Do you see your work as preparations of good works to offer God in the Holy Mass?*

Day 11

# Eucharistic Minds

*Our way of thinking is attuned to the Eucharist, and
the Eucharist in turn confirms our way of thinking.*

–St. Irenaeus

Congratulations! You have made it through the first eleven days!
Beginning tomorrow, and for the eleven days that follow, we
will focus on the saints and the Eucharist. It would be good to
preface our next journey by musing on the Eucharistic minds
of the saints.

There is a theory in psychology that observes that we all have
mental schemas by which we see the world. These are mental
perspectives that structure and shape our thoughts. We can filter
a lot through this perspective. Our perspective becomes the point
of reference for a lot of what we do. We see this very clearly when
people are passionate about a particular hobby or sport. Their
whole lives tend to be organized around these passions. They
choose to wear certain clothes or even decorate their homes or
office spaces with stuff that relates to their hobbies. Their hobby
or sport interests can even dominate their conversations and

influence their weekly activities. The point is, they have mental structures of thought that color their experience of the world.

The saints above all had Eucharistic mindsets. They prioritized the worship of the Lord in the Mass and outside Mass in the tabernacle and intentionally ordered their lives to the Eucharist. Since the Eucharist is the source and summit of our Christian Faith, a saintly mind should be particularly ordered toward the Eucharistic Lord. In acknowledging this fundamental Christian attitude, the *Catechism* quotes the second-century bishop St. Irenaeus: "Our way of thinking is attuned to the Eucharist, and the Eucharist in turn confirms our way of thinking" (CCC, no. 1327). I love this quote because St. Irenaeus is a man of great authority in the Tradition of the Church. He lived very close to those generations of Christians who knew the Lord while He was on earth. We can take seriously His words, which show us the mind of the early Church. It is clearly a Eucharistic mindset. All of Christian life for the early Christians was a life in view of the Eucharist. Nothing has changed for us today.

A few years ago, I was struck by something one of my Dominican brothers said at lunch. He mentioned that he once heard a radio interview with a hermit living in the Dublin mountains. The hermit said his spirituality was the Holy Mass. Everything he did was preparation for Holy Mass and a thanksgiving after it. I was touched by this comment and the hermit's intense intentionality of seeing his whole day as related to the Holy Mass. Hearing that story also reminded me of St. Charbel, a Lebanese hermit, who grew in a deep appreciation for how central and powerful the Holy Mass is for the world. He too would spend hours in preparation for Mass, and spent hours celebrating the Holy Mass itself. He would also spend long hours in Eucharistic Adoration. The same fervent preparation and devotion of adoration can be seen in the lives of St. John Vianney and many other saints. The saints witness to us how our lives should be ordered.

St. Josemaría Escrivá, the founder of Opus Dei, would say his life was a life lived between one Holy Mass and another. He understood that as he left Mass he was already preparing for the next Mass. Bl. Columba Marmion expressed the same rhythm of life in his own words. He spoke of walking in the strength of the Eucharist after Holy Mass throughout the day. He also often commented that he lived off the thought of the Holy Mass and Holy Communion that awaited him the next day.

It is true that most people are not hermits like St. Charbel. Most of us will not have a hermit's time strictly for prayer because we have our own duties of life to fulfill. Nevertheless, the witness of someone like St. Charbel or the hermit in the Dublin mountains is a reminder to us to have the Holy Mass always in mind and to live and act in a manner that allows us to worthily receive the Lord's precious Body into our own bodies. The saints inspire us to true preparation for Mass and thanksgiving after Mass has ended.

We should also note how our daily duties, activities, sacrifices, joys, and thanksgivings are brought with us to Holy Mass. One of the many graces of participating in the Holy Mass is the opportunity to unite ourselves with Jesus' perfect offering of Himself to the Father. In this offering, Jesus, through the priest, perfects and fulfills our offering, giving all our sacrifices and life-offerings a new value. This new value is not something we are capable of lifting up to the Lord unless He transforms it at the Holy Mass. If we really grasp this, then we should see all our lives as a preparation for perfecting our lives in the Holy Mass. Adopting this attitude changes the way we see our most ordinary of human activities. It gives us a Eucharistic mindset through which to see all of our life.

*Let Us Pray:* Lord, help my mind be attuned to the Eucharist. Lord Jesus, remind me throughout the day that my activities are offerings to bring to the altar. Give me the desire to see my life as time spent between one Mass and the next.

## Today's Reflection

*What strikes you most about today's reflection?*

*Do you struggle to have a Eucharistic mind? Is there another mental perspective that dominates your thoughts?*

*What can you do to better prepare to live "from Mass to Mass"?*

Part II

# Days with the Saints

The next eleven days we will spend with the wisdom of the saints.

I remember being struck on my first entrance into St. Peter's Square in Rome. I had this tremendous sense of all the saints embracing me. I then wondered with awe at how Jesus' promise was realized in all their lives. My mind searched all the statues, thinking of the ways God did miracles and astounding acts of love through their lives.

The saints remind me that our Faith is not fiction; it is real. If we are honest with ourselves, most of us are always seeking mentors in life to call us forward to greater heights. We are always looking up to someone to help guide us in this life. The saints stand out as exemplary Christians who found a profound union with God on earth. Their lives manifest the gospel and help us interpret different ways of living a Christian life.

In this section, we will focus on their Eucharistic love, trusting that their words and lives are anointed to enlighten our own hearts. Hopefully, we catch the scent of their souls through their words. We will try to get out of the way and let their words prevail. As a result, they will be quoted at length again and again. I pray we taste their contagious love for our Eucharistic Lord.

# Pope St. John Paul II: The Secret of My Day

*The presence of Jesus in the tabernacle must be a kind of magnetic pole attracting an ever-greater number of souls enamoured of him, ready to wait patiently to hear his voice and, as it were, to sense the beating of his heart.*

—St. John Paul II[29]

"It is pleasant to spend time with him, to lie close to his breast like the Beloved Disciple (cf. Jn 13:25) and to feel the infinite love present in his heart."[30] These are the words of the great St. John Paul II on Eucharistic Adoration. To begin our next eleven days with the saints, I could think of no better saint close to our times whose love for the Eucharist made a tremendous impact on the life of the Church. Along with Pope Benedict XVI and Pope Francis, St. John Paul II made a clarion call for Eucharistic Adoration to spread through the Church. In fact, it was at an

---

[29] Apostolic Letter for the Year of the Eucharist *Mane Nobiscum Domine* (October 7, 2004), no. 18.

[30] Pope John Paul II, *Ecclesia de Eucharistia*, no. 25.

International Eucharistic Congress in Seville, Spain, that St. John Paul II prayed that the fruit of the congress would result "in the establishment of Perpetual Eucharistic Adoration in all parishes and Christian communities throughout the world."

So gripped by the Real Presence of Christ in Eucharistic Adoration, St. John Paul II proclaimed it "the secret of my day." It was such, he said, because "it gives strength and meaning to all my activities of service to the Church and to the whole world."[31] It is no surprise that the pope once wrote: "How can we not feel a renewed need to spend time in spiritual converse, in silent adoration, in heartfelt love before Christ present in the Most Holy Sacrament? How often, dear brother and sisters, have I experienced this, and drawn from it strength, consolation and support!"[32] These are not just words. There are many stories of people finding the pope absorbed in adoration as if he was in the most intense conversation with Christ. There are stories of people finding the saint flat on his face in prostration in his private chapel. He would stay there for many hours at a time.

St. John Paul would have strongly agreed with the candor of St. Edith Stein, one of his favorite saints: "The Lord is present in the tabernacle in his divinity and his humanity.... As a result, anyone with normal thoughts and feelings will naturally be drawn to spend time with him, whenever possible and as much as possible."[33] These words are simple but striking. To want to be near the Eucharistic Lord is a logical consequence for those who know the Lord to be present. Love understands these visits. Some-

---

[31] Pope John Paul II, Address to Young People of Bologna, September 27, 1997.

[32] *Ecclesia de Eucharistia*, no. 25.

[33] St. Teresa Benedicta of the Cross, *Gesammelte Werke*, vol. 7, 136.

thing would be seriously missing in our faith if we "professed" the Eucharistic presence and seldom desired to draw near to Him. The Gospels show us numerous accounts of people wanting to see and be with Jesus in person: "So he ran on ahead and climbed up into a sycamore tree to see him, for he was to pass that way" (Luke 19:4); "Stay with us, for it is toward evening and the day is now far spent" (Luke 24:29); "I will follow you wherever you go" (Luke 9:57); "Sir, we wish to see Jesus" (John 12:21). May these words inspire us!

It is grievous that some see Eucharistic Adoration as a mere devotion among devotions, as if it was just what suits the personal tastes of some. It is not uncommon that people relegate Eucharistic Adoration as a devotion like saying the Rosary or praying the Stations of the Cross or *Lectio Divina*. It is not that these other devotions are not powerful. However, Eucharistic Adoration is not just any devotion. It is not a devotion for a few or for those who "like that kind of thing." In his encyclical on the Eucharist, *Ecclesia de Eucharistia*, St. John Paul quoted St. Alphonsus Liguori as saying, "Of all devotions, that of adoring Jesus in the Blessed Sacrament is the greatest after the sacraments, the one dearest to God and the one most helpful to us."[34] Why is Eucharistic Adoration so powerful and helpful? How can we understand better why the pope's "secret" was so effective for his papacy?

St. John Paul II explained that the reason Eucharistic Adoration is particularly powerful is because it "prolongs and increases the fruits" of Holy Communion. We have already seen in our first eleven days the many fruits of Holy Communion. Imagine now how all these gifts and virtues are maturing and deepening in our time of adoration. We do not simply gaze at the Eucharistic Lord.

---

[34] *Ecclesia de Eucharistia*, no. 25.

He is actively transforming our souls more deeply into himself in adoration. Pope Benedict XVI wrote as Cardinal Ratzinger that Eucharistic Adoration is also a form of eating Christ. He explains that worship is a form of eating. Ratzinger writes of adoration: "Eating it—as we have just said—is a spiritual process, involving the whole man. 'Eating' it means worshipping it. Eating it means letting it come into me, so that my 'I' is transformed and opens up into the great 'we,' so that we become 'one' in Him (cf. Gal 3:16). Thus adoration is not opposed to Communion, nor is it merely added to it."[35] This is a very important point. Eucharistic Adoration is not a mere "add-on" to our spiritual life. By transforming us more into Christ, adoration helps us answer the question: How to be his?

Before we end our reflection today. I would like to highlight the transforming power of Eucharistic Adoration for the world. There is no such thing as private prayer in one sense: Prayer always affects others, whether they (or we) are conscious of it or not. This is because of the Mystical Body of Christ. When one member prays, all benefit. Hence, prayer is the most useful of all human activities, even if we cannot always quantify and measure it. We ought to understand the secret of St. John Paul's day in this sense. His secret wasn't only about him but about the way the Lord used him to affect the whole Church and his ministry.

It can be a temptation to think of Eucharistic Adoration as time that should instead be given to ministry and to others. This would be a great mistake. Such an opinion does not take into account the true power of prayer and its universal effects. St. John Paul II did not consider his hours of daily prayer as negligence of

---

[35] Joseph Cardinal Ratzinger, *The Spirit of the Liturgy* (Ignatius Press, 2000), 90.

his pontificate's duties. He understood it to be its "secret" power. He once wrote to the bishop of Liège:

> Closeness to the Eucharistic Christ in silence and contemplation does not distance us from our contemporaries but, on the contrary, makes us open to human joy and distress, broadening our hearts on a global scale.... Through adoration the Christian mysteriously contributes to the radical transformation of the world and to the sowing of the Gospel. Anyone who prays to the Savior draws the whole world with him and raises it to God.[36]

What a mystery! Adoration draws the whole world to Christ.

*Let Us Pray:* Lord Jesus, raise up saints like Pope John Paul II to help witness to the transformative effects of Eucharistic Adoration. Help me see the Eucharist as the secret of my own day. Give me a heart to intercede on behalf of others to call down your Precious Blood upon their souls.

### Today's Reflection

*Do you have a favorite Gospel passage*
*of people desiring to see Jesus!*

*"Anyone who prays to the Eucharistic Savior draws the*
*whole world with him and raises it to God." Other than*

---

[36] Pope John Paul II, Letter to the Bishop of Liège for the 750th Anniversary of the "Corpus Domini" Festival, May 28 1996, translated passages at "St. Pope John Paul II: Quotes on the Importance of Eucharistic Adoration," St. Francis, T.C., MI, https://stfrancisadoration.org/pope_john_paul_ii.htm.

*yourself, who is most in need of mercy that the Lord is putting on your heart—both locally and around the world?*

*What would you describe as the secret of your day?*

# St. Charles de Foucauld: With Christ in the Desert

*My God, here I am at your feet in my cell. It is night, everything is quiet, everything is sleeping. At this moment I am perhaps the only one in this town at your feet. What have I done to deserve such graces?*

—St. Charles de Foucauld

After rediscovering the Lord and his Catholic Faith, St. Charles de Foucauld famously said, "As soon as I believed that there was a God, I understood that I could do nothing other than to live for him alone."[37] This desire to live for "Him" led St. Charles first to be a Trappist monk and then to become a hermit. Relentlessly pursuing a radical life of poverty and prayer, St. Charles of Jesus eventually built his hermitage in the Sahara Desert. At the heart of his hermitage was the tabernacle. It was at the feet of Jesus that St. Charles experienced adoration of the Blessed Sacrament

---

[37]  Quoted in Antoine Chatelard,  *St. Charles de Foucauld: Journey to Tamanrasset* (Jesus Caritas Publications, 2021), 32.

as "repose, refreshment and joy."[38] He lived from and for the Eucharistic presence of Christ.

St. Charles had a profound sense of the reality of Christ truly coming to him in the Eucharist. In many of his writings you cannot help but feel his wonder and awe at the amazing miracle of the true living Jesus being utterly and wholly present in the Holy Eucharist. There is one quote that captures the simplicity and yet depth of his faith: "Lord Jesus, you are in the Holy Eucharist. You are there, a yard away in the tabernacle. Your body, your soul, your human nature, your divinity, your whole being is there, in its twofold nature. How close you are, my God, my Saviour, my Jesus, my Brother, my Spouse, my Beloved!"[39]

His faith in our Eucharistic Lord was so strong that he didn't see the point of venerating anything else whenever the Lord was present in the Sacrament. He never discounted the power of venerating relics and statues and making pilgrimages to holy places, but he wanted to stress to others that one finds in the Holy Eucharist all of Jesus—He is there completely. In this sense, where else do we want to go? Sometimes we can forget that the Lord Himself waits for us in the Holy Eucharist with open hands to radiate so many blessings on us.

Imagine this hermit alone with our Eucharistic Lord amidst the stars and the great silence of the desert. The beauty of the desert, however, is pale compared to what he finds in the Eucharistic heart of Jesus. On writing of his experience of the Eucharistic Christ in the desert, St Charles notes:

[38] Charles de Foucauld, Letter of January 19, 1903, in *Lettres de Mme de Bondy: de la Trappe à Tamanrasset* (Desclée de Brouwer, 1996).

[39] Jean-Francois Six, ed., *The Spiritual Autobiography of Charles de Foucauld* (Dimension Books, 1964), 98.

Here we are at the gates of eternity. One almost believes that here, looking at these two infinities of the great sky and of the desert. You who like to see the setting of the sun, which, descending sings eternal peace and serenity, you would like seeing the sky and the great horizons of this little fraternity. But the best, the true infinity, the true peace is at the feet of the divine tabernacle. There, no more in an image but in reality, is all our good, our love, our life, our all, our peace, our beatitude: there is all our heart and all our soul, our time and our eternity, our All.[40]

St. Charles finds in the Eucharist not the mere shadow of beauty of the Creator's creation but the source of all beauty and all light, the Creator himself. As he says, in the Eucharist he finds "our All."

Having this sense of "All" in the Eucharist, St. Charles was able to endure the desert silence. For him it was not a suffocating silence but a silence that opened him up to the great abiding presence of the Lord. He once wrote in a letter: "Do not worry yourself seeing me alone, without a friend, without spiritual help: I do not suffer at all from this solitude, I find it very sweet: I have the Blessed Sacrament, the best of friends, to speak to day and night."[41] Amid our own deserts and harsh terrain of life, could we see visits to the Eucharistic Lord as a visit to the One who soothes our heart's deepest ache?

Another very powerful insight St. Charles can offer our Eucharistic meditation is the radiating presence of the Eucharist. St. Charles was so confident in the Eucharistic presence of his

---

[40] Letter of January 19, 1903, in *Lettres de Mme de Bondy.*
[41] Letter of December 16, 1905, in ibid.

best of friends that he saw it as a mission in itself just to set up a tabernacle in an area of Algeria where there was none. He writes in his diary on July 8, 1903: "Sacred Heart of Jesus, thank you for this first tabernacle in Tuareg country. Sacred Heart of Jesus, shine from the heart of this tabernacle upon this people who worship you without knowing you. Enlighten, lead, save these souls that you love." The theme of Jesus "shining" His grace and light is also present in another letter he wrote: "From this tabernacle, Jesus will shine upon these lands and attract adorers to himself.... Does my presence do some good here? If it does not, the presence of the Blessed Sacrament certainly does much: Jesus cannot be in a place without shining."[42]

The notion of the Eucharistic Jesus being an evangelizer, attracting souls to Himself, is a powerful idea. Often we can forget that Jesus Himself just needs to be exposed on an altar, with the doors of the church opened, so He can attract souls to sit at His feet. Jesus is alive in the Eucharist and summons souls to Himself through the promptings and attraction of the Holy Spirit. However, we can act as a barricade to souls coming to Him. We do this if as priests we do not make Jesus available or if as laity or religious we do not encourage people to visit the Lord.

In his catechesis on St. Charles, Pope Francis commented on this idea of the Eucharistic Lord evangelizing. The pope beautifully captures the life and belief of St. Charles:

Charles lets Jesus act silently, convinced that "Eucharistic life" evangelizes. Indeed, he believes that Christ is the first evangelizer. And so he remains in prayer at Jesus' feet, before the Tabernacle, for a dozen hours a day, sure that the

---

[42] Letter of November 18, 1907, in ibid.

evangelizing force resides there and feeling that it is Jesus who will bring him close to so many distant brothers. And do we, I ask myself, believe in the power of the Eucharist? Does our going out to others, our service, find its beginning and its fulfilment there, in adoration?[43]

As we journey these thirty-three days, I pose the pope's question again: Do we believe in the power of the Eucharist?

*Let Us Pray:* Eucharistic Lord, draw me to Yourself. Help me to find in the silence that surrounds your Eucharistic heart the soothing balm for all my longings and aches of loneliness. Help me experience Your presence as refreshment, joy, and peace. Help me see Your Eucharistic heart as the source of all beauty and light in this world.

## Today's Reflection

*What attracts your notice about the words
and life of St. Charles de Foucauld?*

*How has Christ been the "first evangelizer"
for you and your loved ones?*

*Do you find time for solitude to experience
intimacy with Christ?*

---

[43] Pope Francis, General Audience, St. Peter's Square, October 18, 2023.

Day 14

# St. Manuel González García: Eucharistic Eyes

*My faith was looking at Jesus through the
door of that tabernacle, so silent, so patient,
so good, gazing right back at me.*

—St. Manuel González García

Many years ago, I came across a priest preaching about the divine eyes of Jesus buried in the monstrance, studying us from the Sacred Host. Those innocent eyes of our Lord look straight into our souls when we come before Him. He searches our hearts, His Eucharistic gaze bringing us deeper and deeper into prayer.

There is a famous story in the life of the great French mystic and priest, St. John Mary Vianney. He once found a country man sitting for hours looking intently at the tabernacle. Curious about this man, St. John asked him about his long hours of prayer. How did the simple country man spend all that time? "I look at him and he looks at me," was the reply. (I always like to add: "… and we love each other.")

The country man's reply captures contemplative prayer at its best. It is a pondering of the Lord while loving Him, a looking at Him in faith while He looks back at us with love. We often enter the hearts of others through their eyes. It is the same for us with the Lord Jesus.

Today's saint, known as the "bishop of the abandoned tabernacle," was adopted as one of the patrons of the Eucharistic Revival in the United States. Born in Spain, St. Manuel *González García* had a profound experience as a young priest that forever changed his life. It was at a parish mission in rural Spain that the young saint encountered a disheveled, empty church. When he got to the tabernacle, the sanctuary lamp was leaking and there were cobwebs over the tabernacle. The lack of order and tidiness spoke of the people's lack of faith and love for the Real Presence of Christ in the Eucharist.

Overwhelmed and discouraged, Fr. Manuel got on his knees and prayed before the Lord. At that moment, he felt those eyes upon him. He writes: "My faith was looking at Jesus through the door of that tabernacle, so silent, so patient, so good, gazing right back at me.... His gaze was telling me much and asking me for more."[44] It was this moment that transformed his priesthood and drove him to be a great advocate for Eucharistic Adoration, encouraging people never to abandon Jesus' true presence in the tabernacle.

In his writings, St. Manuel has beautiful things to say about this gaze of Jesus. He says, "In the world there are looks of fear, of persecution, of vigilance, of love. How does the heart of Jesus

---

[44] Victoria Schneider, *The Bishop of the Abandoned Tabernacle: St. Manuel González García* (Scepter, 2018), 23.

look at me from the Eucharist?"[45] He goes on to write that "above all his look is not that of a judging eye, like the eye of Cain, the bad brother. It is not the frightened look, of remorse without hope, or of constant judging. No, that isn't how he looks at me now."[46] In another reflection, St. Manuel wonderfully brings alive this gaze of the Eucharistic Jesus:

> The Heart of Jesus in the tabernacle looks at me. He looks at me always. He looks at me everywhere. He looks at me as if he doesn't have anyone else to look at but me. Why?
>
> Because he loves me. When two people love each other they yearn to look at each other. Inquire of the mother who, without talking and barely breathing, spends hours next to her son as he sleeps. Why does she do this? She will answer, "I just want to look at my son."[47]

Have you ever considered the different ways Jesus may gaze on us from the tabernacle? St. Manuel invites us to reflect on three different gazes of Jesus. Each gaze can be an invitation to an examination of conscience under the gaze of Christ

The "first look" is one Jesus gave the rich young man, who said: "Good Teacher, what must I do to inherit eternal life? (Mark 10:17). St. Mark tells us, "And Jesus looking upon him loved him" (Mark 10:21). St. Manuel describes this look as a "gaze of delight, of rest, of gentleness, with which the Heart of Jesus embraces innocent and simple souls, like the young man who had observed the commandments from his youth."[48] St. Manuel says Jesus'

---

[45] Ibid., 58.

[46] Ibid.

[47] Ibid., 57.

[48] Ibid., 59.

gentle gaze also calls for an extra step toward perfection and a greater commitment to the Lord.

The "second look" is like the one Jesus gave Peter after his denial of the Lord in the courtyard of the High Priest. St. Manuel describes the scene:

> There, inside, Jesus is submerged in a sea of ingratitude, cruelty, false accusations ...; outside there is Peter, his closest friend, the trusted man, the confidant of the persecuted Jesus, denying him, once, twice, three times, even with an oath. What happens then? Peter starts to run, holding back the tears which were coming to his eyes. The Prisoner inside, overlooking his own sufferings, directs his gaze back towards the friend who is falling. A gaze filled with memories. A gaze expressing hurt and a broken Heart. A gaze inviting contrition, hope, forgiveness.[49]

It is helpful to imagine this gaze if we visit Jesus and are struggling with some grave sin or addiction. Imagine the eyes of Jesus that cut right to Peter's heart, bringing him back to his senses and to true contrition. What must that gaze of Jesus on Peter have been like? Can we allow this gaze to cut to our own hearts?

The "third look" of Jesus concerns what St. Luke wrote of Jesus lamenting over Jerusalem: "And when he drew near and saw the city he wept over it, saying, 'Would that even today you knew the things that make for peace! But now they are hid from your eyes'" (Luke 19:41–42). Considering this look of Jesus, St. Manuel comments: "It is a desolate look! The Teacher on a mountaintop looked at Jerusalem and wept.... Jesus' hands are tied because of the stubbornness and hardness of that soul

---

[49] Ibid., 59–60.

which frustrates whatever is done to save it. He weeps, as it is the only thing his heart can do."[50] Could we imagine those eyes of Jesus which search our hearts trying to stir up our conversion? Those eyes can stir up our desire to console Jesus for the souls that may be lost daily because they never recognized the visitation of Jesus.

Whatever the state of your soul, the Eucharistic gaze meets you where you are. His gaze is not passive; it calls for more and it empowers us for more. Pope Benedict XVI once said: "When one is overcome by the fire of his gaze, no sacrifice seems too great in order to follow him and to give him the best of oneself."[51] The gaze of Christ purifies us to be the best version of ourselves if we open our hearts to that gaze. Some of the most beautiful words I have ever come across about the gaze of Jesus are also penned by Pope Benedict XVI, in his encyclical *Spe Salvi*, as he explains Purgatory as an encounter with the cleansing gaze of Jesus. He writes:

> Before his gaze all falsehood melts away. This encounter with him, as it burns us, transforms and frees us, allowing us to become truly ourselves. All that we build during our lives can prove to be mere straw, pure bluster, and it collapses. Yet in the pain of this encounter, when the impurity and sickness of our lives become evident to us, there lies salvation. His gaze, the touch of his heart heals us through an undeniably painful transformation "as through fire." But it is a blessed pain, in which the holy

---

[50]  Ibid., 60.
[51]  Pope Benedict XVI, Address to Young People of the Archdiocese of Madrid, April 2, 2012.

power of his love sears through us like a flame, enabling us to become totally ourselves and thus totally of God.[52]

It is the same Jesus who gazes on us from the Eucharist that a soul meets in Purgatory. The difference is His gaze is hidden and quiet in Eucharistic Adoration. Nevertheless, Eucharistic Adoration has the power to help us become our true selves as the Eucharistic Christ actively gazes on us, working deeply in our souls in the power of the Holy Spirit to help us shed our false selves. Right under his gaze, we have the potential to become "born again" into our deepest identity. We can return to our deepest and truest heart.

*Let Us Pray:* Lord, I want to discover Your Eucharistic eyes. May Your gaze rest upon my heart. Melt the hardness of my heart. May Your light dispel any falsehood and plant in me authentic desires to follow You and do Your will. Give me the faith I need to see Your face in the Eucharist so I can gaze back with love.

## Today's Reflection

*How have you experienced Jesus' gazing upon you from the Tabernacle? What kind of gaze was it?*

*"When a person is conquered by the fire of his gaze, no sacrifice seems too great to follow him and give*

---

[52] Pope Benedict XVI, Encyclical Letter on Christian Hope *Spe Salvi* (November 30, 2007), no. 47, https://www.vatican.va /content/benedict-xvi/en/encyclicals/documents/hf_ben-xvi _enc_20071130_spe-salvi.html.

*him the best of ourselves." Have you experienced
Jesus' Eucharistic gaze as a source of strength?*

*Have you ever noticed the movements of your
heart changing after long prayer with Christ?
Do you ever feel more authentically yourself
when you spend time with Christ?*

# St. Manuel González García: How He Speaks and Listens

*Have we ever considered the fact that there is Someone who speaks and works with power hidden in the tabernacle?*

—St. Manuel González García

Yesterday we considered with St. Manuel the eyes of Jesus, gazing at us from the Eucharist. Today we will consider His Eucharistic mouth and ears: From the tabernacle, Jesus speaks and listens.

Our Spanish saint does not shy away from the realism of Christ in the Eucharist. The Eucharist is not some container of Christ's presence; it is truly Jesus, with all His biological senses and personality sacramentally present. Reflecting on the Eucharistic voice of Jesus, St. Manuel says:

Here is a question that will perplex many Christians and probably even a few pious people too. What does Jesus do and say [from the tabernacle]? Have we ever considered the fact that there is Someone who speaks and works with power hidden in the tabernacle?... I would be very happy if Christians who read these words arise determined to go to the tabernacle to see what is done and to hear what is said there by the most good and constant of lovers.... I tell you that there is no place on earth with activity more fruitful than that which is done in the tabernacle. It is not for the eye or the ear of the flesh to perceive these things, but for the ear and eye of the soul.[53]

Do we listen deeply to the Eucharistic Jesus in our time of prayer, confident that He speaks? Pope St. John Paul II often said: "Let Jesus present in the Blessed Sacrament speak to your hearts." He once exhorted a group of people to understand that in the "silence of the white Host, carried in the ostensory, are all his words; there is his whole life given in offering to the Father for each of us."[54] Do we hear His words?

The Tradition of the Church invites us to be confident that we can. Pastoral experience confirms that He speaks. You need only to ask those who frequent Eucharistic Adoration. They will tell you of their experience with Christ. Sometimes there is just a deep listening to the fact that He is present. Other times He prompts the heart interiorly with His words. Having said this, how do we hear Him? How do we enter His heart? St. Manuel asks: "Do we have to go to special revelations granted to special souls? Do we have to look for miracles or extraordinary manifestations of God hidden in the tabernacle? Who is going to reveal to us those treasures of beauty and their marvels?"[55]

---

[53] Schneider, *Bishop of the Abandoned Tabernacle*, 45–48.

[54] Pope John Paul II, Angelus, June 17, 1979, no. 1, https://www.vatican.va/content/john-paul-ii/en/angelus/1979/documents/hf_jp-ii_ang_19790617.html.

[55] Schneider, *Bishop of the Abandoned Tabernacle*, 51.

St. Manuel speaks of the great revealer of the tabernacle, who is going to help us discover the marvels of His voice and converse with us. It is worth quoting him at length:

> It is now time to unveil the great revealer of the tabernacle, the great confidant, the intimate friend who can grant us access to that palace of mysterious marvels that is the tabernacle. Are you in a hurry to know who it is? Its name is … the Gospel! This is the powerful finger that is going to lift the veil from our eyes so we can discover these secrets.[56]

St. Manuel calls the Gospels the "messenger the Good God sent us so that our eyes and our ears of flesh could see and listen to what is said and done in the tabernacle."[57] As a result there is no "need of miracles or special revelations."

The Sacred Tradition of the Church has always seen itself along with the Sacred Scriptures as the primary means by which we hear the living voice of God. The Lord has chosen to reveal Himself to the world through Catholic Tradition and Scripture. When we ponder the Scriptures in faith, the Word of God leads us to true knowledge of the Lord. The four Gospels have a special place in all of Scripture because they help us come to know the true personality of Christ. This same personality is present in the Eucharist. The Jesus of the Gospels is the same Jesus before us in the Eucharist. He is there with His entire personality. This is why the Gospel is the best companion we can carry with us in our time of Eucharistic Adoration. It is the key to unlock our ears to hear Christ speaking in the Eucharist. We need only invite the Holy Spirit whose role it is to reveal Jesus and His voice to

---

[56] Ibid.
[57] Ibid.

us. The Holy Spirit brings God's word alive in our soul in deep prayer. It is important to invoke the Holy Spirit as we await His voice in the Eucharist and in the Scriptures.

The fact that Jesus is speaking to us in adoration is only one side of the coin. The other side is that Jesus actively listens to us. Isn't it consoling that in the tabernacle, Jesus still makes special audiences with every disciple of every age? We can go to Him and unburden all our anxieties. We can tell Him all our joys and plans. The Eucharistic Lord is listening even if we are too weary to pray and say anything. Just by being with Him, we allow Him to listen to the unspoken words of our hearts. If we feel broken and in bondage, sometimes it is enough to go before the Lord like the leper and pray with faith, "Lord, heal me!"

Interestingly, St. Manuel makes a distinction between Jesus listening and Jesus hearing: "Notice that I don't say 'hear,' but 'listen,' which means to hear with interest, with attention, with gladness. And then I add the word 'always.' These are three things that nobody in the world does: to listen always, to listen to everyone, and to listen to everything."[58] Jesus, however, does all three. Would it change your prayer if you became very conscious that the Eucharistic Lord is waiting to listen deeply with love and respect to your heart? Know that Jesus' eyes, mouth, and ears are present in the Host. He gazes, speaks, and listens.

> *Let Us Pray*: Lord, I long to hear Your voice in adoration.
> Teach me to recognize it. Please open the Scriptures to me
> in Your presence like You did for the disciples on the road
> to Emmaus. Help me discover Your voice in the Gospels.
> Teach me there about Your personality. I want to hear who

[58] Ibid., 68.

You are with all my being. Jesus, help me be aware that You listen deeply to my own heart.

## Today's Reflection

*Have you given much thought to the fact that Jesus in the Eucharist has ears to listen to your heart? How does this knowledge affect your desire for prayer?*

*The Gospel helps us hear God's voice and encounter Christ fully in adoration. This week, choose a Gospel passage—perhaps John 6 or one of the healing miracles—and ask the Lord to reveal His heart to you through His Word.*

*Jesus waits and listens to us patiently. How can you imitate this in your own life with someone in need of a listening ear?*

# St. Thomas Aquinas: Eating Light

*I am the light of the world;*
*he who follows me will not walk in darkness,*
*but will have the light of life.*

—John 8:12

The Eucharist is the food of divine wisdom. In his apostolic constitution *Vultum Dei Quaerere* (Seeking the Face of God), Pope Francis remarks that "The Church draws her life from Christ in the Eucharist; she is fed by him and by him she is enlightened."[59] We have already explored in our first eleven days how the Eucharist increases Christ's love in us. It is left for us to muse on how the Eucharist makes us wise with the light of Christ. It is truly astonishing that we actually have something

---

[59] Pope Francis, Apostolic Constitution on Women's Contemplative Life *Vultum Dei Quaerere* (June 29, 2016), no. 22, https://www.vatican.va/content/dam/francesco/pdf/apost_constitutions/documents/papa-francesco_costituzione-ap_20160629_vultum-dei-quaerere_en.pdf.

on earth to eat that can help us grow in wisdom and light. We have something on earth that we can adore, and in adoring we can grow in enlightenment. Of course, this "something" is a "someone," our Eucharistic Lord. St. Thomas Aquinas will help us think out this great mystery today.

Isn't it interesting that Eve tried to grow in wisdom by eating something? The book of Genesis says: "So when the woman saw that the tree was good for food, and that it was a delight to the eyes, and that the tree was to be desired to make one *wise*, she took of its fruit and ate; and she also gave some to her husband, and he ate" (Gen. 3:6, emphasis added). The fact that the human race fell by trying to eat wisdom on its own terms is significant, because there is a "fruit" offered freely in the Church, a fruit that no market or business can trade. It is not the forbidden fruit that Eve grasped as she tried to grow in divine wisdom; it is the fruit of the tree of the Cross, the fruit who is Wisdom Himself, Jesus Christ. As the bride of the New Adam, Christ, the Church offers this fruit to us to undo what Eve offered to her husband Adam. Catholics could be stirred to greater Eucharistic devotion if they were reminded that they can grow in light and truth through the faithful reception of Holy Communion and adoration of the Blessed Sacrament.

Every saint's life is remembered by a host of legends and memories. Some are true and some are myths that speak about a truth that the saint embodied. From the investigations that prepared St. Thomas Aquinas's canonization, there is a captivating image of the saint from Reginald of Piperno. Bishop Robert Barron says that Reginald "was convinced" that St. Thomas's "wisdom came much more from the intensity of his prayer than the diligence of his study." Interestingly, Bishop Barron says that Reginald concluded this from "frequently" seeing St. Thomas "resting his head against the tabernacle, lost in contemplation, especially when he was wrestling with a particularly thorny theological problem."[60] Why would St. Thomas go to the tabernacle if it was not for the Eucharistic light that radiates from Christ's heart? This is not a nice pious gesture on St. Thomas's part. His theology taught him that, hidden in the Eucharistic grace, is a bright spark of light. The Eucharistic Lord was the place where he knew he could draw the hidden wisdom of the eternal Word.

To better understand the wisdom light of the Eucharist, we need to unpack the meaning of sanctifying grace and what it means to be sanctified. St. Thomas points out that sanctifying grace is not simply some deposit of "divine stuff" in our soul. It is the transformation of our soul in God, causing special divine gifts to unfold and transforming the soul's powers of knowing and loving. Sanctifying grace heals our intellects and wills from the effects of sin and elevates them to start sharing in the Trinity's way of knowing and loving. On its own, without grace, our capacity to know and love in a divine way is impossible. We need grace. However, as we grow in grace, our minds are filled with a brighter light, enabling a more intimate knowledge of the triune God and a deeper understanding of all that Christ has divinely revealed. The secrets of Heaven are shared with the soul.

St. Thomas taught that at the heart of sanctifying grace is the unfolding of two principal gifts in the soul: love and wisdom. Each gift is unique in the way that it makes us share in God's way of knowing and loving, thus making the soul like the Blessed

---

[60] Robert Barron, *Exploring Catholic Theology: Essays on God, Liturgy, and Evangelization* (Baker Academic, 2015), 131.

Trinity. The grace of love (charity) mystically likens and unites us to the Holy Spirit, who proceeds in love from the Father and the Son. The gift of wisdom likens and unites us to Christ the Word, who proceeds from the Father in all eternity as Divine Wisdom. Regarding this latter gift St. Thomas writes: "Now men are called the children of God in so far as they participate in the likeness of the only-begotten and natural Son of God ... who is Wisdom Begotten. Hence by participating in the gift of wisdom, man attains to the sonship of God."[61] In other words, when a soul grows in wisdom, the image of Jesus comes to fulfilment in the soul because Jesus is the Wisdom of God.

Doesn't this shed light on the nature of our divine sonship in Christ? Our identity as sons and daughters of God is marked above all by the degrees of our sharing in God's wisdom. The more we grow in wisdom, the more we resemble a child of God. This sharing, however, is not a sharing in some cold intellectual insight. It is a loving, intimate knowledge of the Father as revealed and experienced in Christ.

The relevance of these truths for our reflection today is that St. Thomas taught that the Eucharist is the source par excellence of our mystical growth and transformation in Christ's divine life on earth. There is no more powerful source of sanctifying grace than our Eucharistic Lord. The Eucharistic Lord will impart to us the gifts of both wisdom and love necessary to produce in our souls a more radiant share in the knowledge and love of Christ. This is what St. Thomas understood and helps us understand. It explains why he often placed his head on the tabernacle in adoration, searching for light and insight. Recall what St. John Paul

---

[61] St. Thomas Aquinas, *Summa Theologiae* II–II, q. 45, art. 6.

II taught us a few days ago: Eucharistic Adoration prolongs and intensifies the graces of Holy Communion. This means that St. Thomas knew from experience that Eucharistic Adoration was a true means of prolonging and intensifying the gift of wisdom that he received in Holy Communion.

Let us conclude. Ever since the Garden of Eden, humanity has been searching for wisdom, and like Eve, has been tempted to find it in disordered ways. The desire for light, a well-accepted image for knowledge and wisdom, has not been erased from the human heart. Humanity is still looking for the fruit that Eve stole. We are trying to get wise on our own terms and as a result are falling into deeper darkness. Pastoral experience shows that when people are taught that Christ is offering the fruit of Himself as the divine light, a fruit which can make them wise, this truth resonates deeply in their hearts. It is as if some primal instinct from our first parents to eat divine wisdom is now finally at rest in its true place in Christ's Eucharistic heart.

*Let Us Pray*: Lord, I want to eat Your light. Increase my hunger for Your Eucharistic light. Help me understand that Your Eucharistic heart is the source of the greatest light for my mind on earth. Please illuminate my mind in adoration and Holy Communion to new levels, so I may see and perceive You more clearly in my life. May this drive me to greater love of You and neighbor.

## Today's Reflection

*St. Thomas Aquinas possessed one of the finest
theological minds of the Church, and yet he recognized
his need for the "divine light" of the Eucharist. Where
do you need that divine light in your life today?*

*Are you in the habit of consciously seeking divine
wisdom in the Eucharist? Does today's teaching
stir your desire for the bread of wisdom?*

*Did you ever think that your growth
in divine wisdom is a key feature that
makes you resemble Christ?*

Day 17

# St. Peter Julian Eymard:
# The Apostle of the Eucharist

*There is nothing greater or holier we can
do on earth than this adoration.*

—St. Peter Julian Eymard

Today's saint gave himself completely to preaching and writing about the Eucharist. Pope St. John XXIII called him the "Apostle of the Eucharist," and canonized him in front of many bishops of the world during the Second Vatican Council. Such a gesture by the Church suggests that Divine Providence chose St. Peter Julian Eymard's eucharistic love and writings as a universal model for disciples everywhere. Today we will focus on how he understood Eucharistic Adoration to be the holiest of actions after the Holy Mass itself.

It is very clear in St. Peter Julian's Eucharistic theology that the greatest act of religion is the solemn worship of God through the offering of the Holy Sacrifice of the Mass. He thought that there could be nothing greater for God's glory than to participate in the Holy Mass. The Holy Mass supersedes every other kind of prayer. It is within this context we have to understand his comment on Eucharistic Adoration: "There is nothing greater or holier we can do on earth than this adoration. Eucharistic adoration is the greatest of actions. . . . To adore is to share the life of the saints in heaven who never cease to praise, bless, and adore the goodness, the love, the glory, the power, and the divinity of the Lamb immolated for the love of men and the glory of God the Father."[62] The saint is not putting the worship of our Eucharistic Lord outside of Mass as something greater. Instead, his spiritual insight penetrates to the profound link between the adoration offered to the Lord through the Holy Mass and the adoration of Our Lord in the Eucharist "outside of" Mass.

Having said this, let us look at some other reasons why St. Peter Julian considers Eucharistic Adoration as the holiest of actions after the Holy Mass itself. For him, Eucharistic Adoration of Our Lord in the tabernacle or in the monstrance requires the perfect exercise of all the virtues in us. St. Peter Julian first begins with the virtue of faith, because faith is the foundation of the spiritual life. He writes that "faith is complete and perfect" when we adore Jesus Christ "hidden, veiled, and as it were, annihilated in the Sacred Host." This hiddenness of the Lord calls forth in us a complete "adoration through all our faculties, all our senses, out of a pure spirit of faith."[63] While every prayer requires faith, the adoration of the Eucharist requires us to go a step further in faith to believe that what looks like bread is actually the Savior and Creator of the whole world. Every act of Eucharistic Adoration,

---

[62] St. Peter Julian Eymard, *In the Light of the Monstrance*, Eymard Library, vol. 9 (Emmaus Publishing, 1940), 177.
[63] Ibid., 178.

therefore, helps us make a profound act of faith which perfects the spiritual life in us.

Now besides faith, our spiritual life is also perfected in hope and in acts of love. St. Peter Julian comments that "since love is the whole law, we fulfil the whole law when, according to the first commandment, we adore our Lord and God." He goes on to say that when we adore we also fulfill the commandment to love others because "we can, in adoration, practice perfect charity towards our neighbor by praying for him, by becoming mediators, victims for his salvation."[64] The point is that Eucharistic Adoration is a school of love. When we adore in love, we reach the summit of Christian perfection.

Throughout his writings, St. Peter Julian also emphasizes how adoration perfects other virtues in us, such as humility, patience, courage, purity of heart, and many more. Adoration calls for a great act of humility, since we have to kneel with humility before the Lord. It also requires patience to sit for a long time in adoration before Jesus. The word *patience* comes from the Latin word that implies suffering. We have to suffer many distractions and false desires that can rage in us to pull us away from adoration.

How many times do we feel so many other seemingly pressing desires to stop us from going to adoration? To overcome these desires we need courage against the temptations that want to sidetrack our desire to visit and adore the Lord. Even when we have committed to do a holy hour, it takes spiritual courage to resist the dryness and boredom that can be thrown up to us by the evil one and also our fallen human nature. The adorer must exercise great virtue in order to fight the evil in the heart that

---

[64] Ibid.

wants to rebel against those precious moments with Jesus in the Eucharist. When we do frequent adoration, it means we are perfecting the virtues in us to help us overcome the vices that can threaten our time of prayer.

Another great insight of St. Peter Julian concerns how the Eucharistic Lord models different virtues to us. It is best to hear the insight in his own words:

> Few persons think of the virtues, the life, the state of our Lord in the Blessed Sacrament. We treat Him like a statue; we think He is there merely to forgive our sins and to listen to our prayers. That is a wrong viewpoint. Our Lord lives and acts in the Eucharist. Look at Him, study, and imitate Him.... Observe him practicing virtue, and you shall know what you have to do.... All our virtues must come from the Eucharist.[65]

In adoration we ought therefore to consider the humility of Christ in coming to us in such a humble state in the Eucharist. St. Peter Julian says: "In the Eucharist, Jesus makes humility His royal virtue. It is the form of all His actions."[66] There is no spectacular phenomenon around the Eucharist. Instead, we contemplate a humble, still, white Host. St. Peter Julian sees in the host the humility and poverty of Christ that is the continuation of the Bethlehem mystery and all the mysteries of Jesus' life which signify His humility and poverty. What perhaps expresses His humility so clearly is the patience of Christ in the Eucharist. St. Peter says, "Patience and forgiveness He still practices in a higher

---

[65] Ibid., 39–41.
[66] Ibid., 75.

degree than on Calvary. There His executioners knew Him not; here they know Him, and yet insult Him."[67]

The very silence of Christ in the Eucharist is also another virtue worth considering. It challenges us to refrain from engaging in useless chatter, or speaking unnecessarily to attract attention. Jesus in the Eucharist simply *is*. He can help us remember to be quiet and silent to create space for other people in our lives. We often talk over others. Jesus in this mystery of silence teaches us to be attentive to others and to the Father in silence.

St. Peter Julian also considers the purity of Christ in the Eucharist: "Jesus is the essence of purity itself in the Eucharist: so pure that He unites Himself with no substance, not even that of bread."[68] The point is that the Eucharist calls us to contemplate and imitate the purity of Christ. It is said that purity means to be of one thing. The Eucharist is one thing—it is completely Christ. Purity has also been described as willing one thing, God's will. Purity, therefore, is more than just sexual purity; it is to be totally devoted to God, aligning our will with His. It is to have purity of intention in all we do.

Another great virtue the Eucharistic Jesus calls us to imitate is obedience. St. Peter Julian believed that the Eucharist shows us the most perfect obedience of Christ. He says that at Holy Mass the Eucharist is consecrated by the action of the priest. Hence, the Son of God comes to the altar "obedient" to the action and words of the priest. Similarly, the saint makes the point that "He comes to you when you wish: you choose the hour, you yourself measure your dispositions, you present yourself and He is already

---

[67] St. Peter Julian Eymard, *The Real Presence* (Fathers of the Blessed Sacrament, 1907), 238.

[68] Eymard, *Light of the Monstrance*, 80.

there" in the Eucharist. St. Peter Julian marvels over this "obedience" of Jesus.

The Eucharist also models to us the great availability and generosity of Christ to the soul. He is ever present and hospitable to all who come to Him. He is waiting silently to listen to our hearts and problems. He gives us His full attention. This is something we can learn in our interactions with others. The Eucharistic Lord calls us to imitate His complete attention to others.

Both availability and generosity speak to another virtue, love. The Eucharistic Christ models great love for us in gifting us His very self and presence. He is always willing to give us all by giving us Himself. He makes Himself present so that He can comfort us in our hour of greatest need. He is so merciful to us, knowing we need His tangible presence. Doesn't this in turn teach us to be there for those in their hour of need?

The Eucharistic heart of Christ also can teach us about meekness and kindness. In the Eucharist, Jesus appears to us in a very gentle and kind way, inviting us to the same virtues. He veils his glory so we can approach Him with confidence and not fear. His gentleness helps us open our hearts to Him despite our sinfulness. He patiently waits for us.

Brothers and sisters, we must consider the state in which the Eucharistic Christ comes to us. Let us conform our minds to the great lesson of love, obedience, humility, patience, gentleness, generosity, and availability in which He instructs us from His Eucharistic heart. In fact, so many other virtues can be found in the Eucharist if we but stop to contemplate them. Let us contemplate that Jesus not only comes with grace but also as a model of truthful living. We can end with these words of St. Peter Julian: "Only in the Eucharist is the truth of Jesus perfectly understood; the disciples of Emmaus knew the saviour in the 'breaking of the Bread.' Divine truth receives its supreme grace in the Holy Eucharist; it is Jesus Who speaks in It, Who reveals It, Who manifests Himself. Certainly no light can compete with the Sun."[69] Jesus in the Eucharist continues to shine as a radiant model of the virtuous life.

*Let Us Pray:* Lord, open the eyes of my heart to see all the virtues of life that You are living now in the Eucharist. Help me imitate You.

## Today's Reflection

*Have you ever contemplated the virtues
of Jesus in the Eucharist?*

*Which Eucharistic virtue speaks most to you? Can
you think of one we did not mention today?*

*What temptations do you most often encounter
to distract you from going to adoration? How
can this be an opportunity for virtue?*

[69] Ibid., 118.

Day 18

# St. Pier Giorgio Frassati: Toward the Heights

*Feed on this Bread of the Angels from which you
will draw the strength to fight inner struggles.*

—St. Pier Giorgio Frassati

The witness of the saints is contagious. Their lives are anointed
to inspire our own. Hopefully you have been inspired so far in
these days by walking with the saints and catching a scent of their
Eucharistic love. Today we shall meet the recently canonized lay
Dominican St. Pier Giorgio Frassati. His fervent devotion has
drawn many young people to our Eucharistic Lord.

Born in 1901 in Turin, Italy, Pier Giorgio Frassati loved going
with his friends up the mountains. If time allowed, it is said that
he would spend entire days in the mountains, contemplating the
greatness of the Creator. One of his personal mottos was *"verso
l'alto"* (toward the heights). With this phrase he would encourage
others not to settle for spiritual mediocrity but to struggle onward
to the heights of holiness. For Pier, mountains were a great symbol of the ascent of the spiritual life to union with God. While

climbing a mountain involves struggle and toil, one is rewarded with the bright sunshine and the freshness of the pure air. The same is true of our life of prayer with Christ. To have the discipline to pray can be both toil and struggle up the mountain of Christ. The fruit of prayer, however, is the joy and spiritual energy that gushes forth from coming into contact with the light of Christ. This light rejuvenates our spirits.

Without a doubt the Eucharist was the source and summit of Pier Giorgio's prayer journey "to the heights." He often encouraged others to go to the Blessed Sacrament. He knew the energizing love of our Eucharistic Lord from personal experience. Speaking from his own inner conviction on July 29, 1923, to a group of Catholic young people in Pollone, he said, "I urge you with all the strength of my soul to approach the Eucharistic Table as often as possible. Feed on this Bread of the Angels from which you will draw the strength to fight inner struggles, the struggles against passions and against all adversities, because Jesus Christ has promised to those who feed themselves with the most Holy Eucharist, eternal life and the necessary graces to obtain it."[70]

The power of Holy Communion, therefore, was not something theoretical for Pier Giorgio; he lived it and experienced it. It is why he could say, "Jesus is with me. I have nothing to fear." His own sister Luciana wrote about the effect of the Eucharist in her brother's life: "The power of Christ working in him every morning is the only explanation we can give to particular heroic acts of self-sacrifice and of charity, to his enormous spirit of humility, and to the moral astuteness of his life."[71]

---

[70] Quoted in "His Eucharistic Devotion," Frassati USA, accessed June 10, 2025, https://frassatiusa.org/his-eucharistic-devotion.
[71] Ibid.

Other witnesses speak more directly about seeing him in Eucharistic prayer. Noticing his reverence, one priest said: "Behold a new young saint who cannot remain far from Heaven much longer." There is also a beautiful testimony from another priest, Fr. Tommaso Castagno:

> I remember Pier Giorgio well during adoration one night in the Turin cathedral: he was kneeling on the floor trying to pray as other young people were brushing past him as they went to and from Communion. Melted wax dripped from the candles onto his suitcoat, and he didn't seem to notice it at all, so absorbed was he in his prayers. Then I understood what Communion and a Eucharistic life meant to him.[72]

Another witness, Attilio Amedeo, knew Pier Giorgio and saw him in deep states of prayer during Holy Communion. Attilio had this to say:

> I would see Pier Giorgio in church every morning, going to Communion and praying, always kneeling in his pew, so absorbed, so concentrated on what he was doing that I was sure that he wouldn't have been disturbed if a bee would have stung him.
>
> Every time I saw him going to the altar to receive Communion, the thought occurred to me that one day I would like to attain his purity of spirit, so that I could receive the Sacrament with the same enthusiasm and intensity.[73]

---

[72] Ibid.
[73] Ibid.

Attilio was also inspired by his witness of thanksgiving after Mass, a practice that sadly has been abandoned by many of the Catholic faithful. Attilio comments: "I noticed how he faithfully spent a long time making his thanksgiving after Holy Communion, praying with such fervor that I was amazed."[74] These testimonies are important for us to grasp the testimonial power of our own Eucharistic love upon others. As a parish or any ecclesial community, we have a sacred duty to witness to each other the living Eucharistic presence of Jesus in our midst. One of the greatest testimonies we can offer each other is to stay behind after Mass has ended to linger in the deeper union the Eucharist has wrought in our souls with Christ.

One of the powerful metaphors St. Pier Giorgio also used to explain his experience of the Eucharist was that of fire. For him, the Eucharistic Lord was not only a source of strength but also a cleansing fire which helped him burn up his defects and acquire true peace and purity of heart. He said,

> When you are totally consumed by the Eucharistic fire, then you will be able more consciously to thank God, who has called you to become part of His family. Then you will enjoy the peace that those who are happy in this world have never experienced, because true happiness, oh young people, does not consist in the pleasures of this world, or in earthly things, but in peace of conscience, which we only have if we are pure of heart and mind.[75]

[74] Ibid.

[75] Quoted in Olivia Spears, "Blessed Pier Giorgio Frassati Quotes," *To the Heights*, March 3, 2018, https://totheheights.com/2609 /bl-pier-giorgio-frassati-quotes/.

In a real sense, this peace of conscience is really to return to the healthy mind and heart that is not conflicted and disturbed by sin. The cleansing fire of Eucharistic grace helps fortify our true self in Christ.

This Eucharistic fire was not something limited to Holy Communion. St. Pier Giorgio also knew this fire in the hours spent in Eucharistic Adoration outside of Mass. So often he drew spiritual energy and strength from time at the feet of Jesus in the tabernacle. There he often found himself lost in the heart of Christ. Pier Giorgio's life testifies to his own experience of the transforming effects of the Eucharist. I have no doubt he would find an echo of his life in the words of St. Paul to the Corinthians: "And we all, with unveiled face, beholding the glory of the Lord, are being changed into his likeness from one degree of glory to another; for this comes from the Lord who is the Spirit" (2 Cor. 3:18).

Commenting on this verse of St. Paul, Ven. Fulton Sheen fleshes out what St. Pier Giorgio experienced in the Eucharist. Sheen powerfully testifies to the effect of Eucharistic Adoration in these words:

> We become like that which we gaze upon. Looking into a sunset, the face takes on a golden glow. Looking at the Eucharistic Lord for an hour transforms the heart in a mysterious way as the face of Moses was transformed after his companionship with God on the mountain. Something happens to us similar to that which happened to the disciples at Emmaus. On Easter Sunday afternoon when the Lord met them, he asked why they were so gloomy. After spending some time in His presence, and hearing again the secret of spirituality—"the Son of Man must suffer to

enter into His Glory"—their time with Him ended and their "hearts were on fire."[76]

Before we end today's reflection, it is important to recall what was said in our first eleven days. For the Eucharistic fire to truly transform us, we must come close to Jesus with the right dispositions of heart: faith, hope, and love. We need not feel on top of the world with a robust faith. Even a small act of faith releases untold graces from Christ's heart into our own. What matters is that we humble ourselves in His presence, trusting that Jesus will act on us. No one ever comes to Jesus with faith, hope, and love and leaves empty-handed. It is not "possible" for the Lord to see us in this state and not be moved in compassion to help us. The Gospels teach us this. Jesus is not a stoic! Thank God. The experience of Eucharistic adorers teaches us this. This Eucharistic prayer is a fast track to holiness.

> *Let Us Pray:* Lord, I call upon the intercession of St. Pier Giorgio Frassati to help me see the Eucharist as the source of my growth in holiness in this life. May I experience the same commitment and love for Your Eucharistic presence as he did. Help me draw strength for my own struggles from Your Eucharistic heart. Lord, I want to be a saint; please help me.

---

[76] Fulton J. Sheen, *A Treasure in Clay: The Autobiography of Fulton J. Sheen* (1980; repr., Image Books, 2008), 198.

## Today's Reflection

*What inspires you most about the story and
testimony of St. Pier Giorgio Frassati?*

*Can you think of someone in your life whose witness
of prayer and Eucharistic love inspires you?*

*Are you in the habit, like Pier Giorgio, of staying behind
after Mass has ended and lingering in thanksgiving?*

Day 19

# St. John of the Cross:
# The Little Host So Close to Us



*This living spring that I long for, I see in this
bread of life, although it is night.*

—St. John of the Cross

"I am the door. If any one enters by me, he will be saved and will
go in and out and find pasture" (John 10:9). We often have to
pass through the narrow gate to enter into the broad and verdant
pastures of holiness. We have to renounce much to attain the
single pearl of great price, God our all. We have to recollect and
focus our minds and hearts on the Lord Jesus to perceive His
all-surpassing abundance. We have to go beyond the diversion
of many distractions to sink into the "one thing necessary," and
it is bottomless.

The Eucharistic Host we adore is small. Our focus in adoration is single-eyed. Yet within the mystery of the Eucharist is a
vast universe expanding beyond all imagination. The narrow
gate of the Eucharist opens up to wide-open green and verdant

pastures where the Lord guides us to springs of living water (see Rev. 7:17).

Our saint today, St. John of the Cross, can inspire us to see in the Eucharist the hidden spring of eternal life. St. John of the Cross was captivated by the expansive transcendence of the mystery of God in the Eucharist. He can help us awaken our own awe and wonderment over the vast terrain of the Eucharistic heart of Christ. Knowing that breadth, length, height, and depth of Christ's love that surpasses all knowing was St. John of the Cross's holy obsession (see Eph. 3:18–19). He sought the eternal flow of divine life gushing forth in the processions of Son and Spirit from the Father, mightier than any waterfall, a boundless love that our souls stretch out and reach for in the limitless heights above. And this St. John of the Cross finds precisely in the Eucharistic Host. He writes: "That eternal spring is hidden, for I know well where it has its rise, although it is night.... I know well that it is bottomless and no one is able to cross it, although it is night.... This eternal spring is hidden in this living bread for our life's sake, although it is night.... This living spring that I long for, I see in this bread of life, although it is night."[77]

What remains hidden in the night, St. John sees in this Bread of Life, in the small and simple Host. The narrow gate of the Eucharist opens up to the transcendent mystery of God's unbounded love. And we get to see it in God's love becoming so humble and little for us in the Host, precisely out of His infinite love for us. The transcendent trinitarian gushing forth of divine life is so close to us in the Eucharist that despite its mystery John calmly

---

[77] St. John of the Cross, "Song of the Soul" from *Dark Night of the Soul* (Dover Publications, 2003).

says he knows it well! "For I know well the spring that flows and runs, although it is night."[78]

Before the Eucharist, in the adoration chapel, we really *adore*. Adoring the immense mystery of God means perceiving His utter transcendence in the Host. The weight of God's presence ought to bring us to our knees. Although it is a dark night at times and we see only through faith, we know the mystery well even as it eludes our grasp.

In the midst of our busy and complicated lives, we need the simplicity and focus of the adoration chapel. But even this "holy habit" can become rote and routine. We need to realize anew, as if for the first time, the grandeur of the mystery present in the Eucharist. It can be a challenge at times to gather ourselves together and return to Our Lord, our center-point, with hearts awake. Yet silent longing draws us to this place of awakened love.

We need to take the time in silence and stillness for the immense mystery that we adore to open up before us, to lose ourselves through this little Host into the bottomless mystery and spring of life gushing forth in the Eucharistic Host.

From another angle, St. John describes an ache born in his adoration as the Eucharist opens up his desire for the final vision of God in Heaven, a vision he cannot yet have. "When I try to find relief seeing you in the Sacrament, I find this greater sorrow: All things are affliction since I do not see you as I desire, and I die because I do not die."[79] Although he finds the spring of divine

---

[78] St. John of the Cross, "Song of the Soul."

[79] See St. John of the Cross, *Spiritual Canticle*, stanza 7, in *A Spiritual Canticle of the Soul and the Bridegroom Christ*, trans. David Lewis (1909; CCEL,1995), https://ccel.org/ccel/john_cross/canticle /canticle.iv.html.

life hidden in Christ's Eucharistic heart, he languishes over the fact that this spring is veiled and hidden. It is as if the Eucharistic veil is a "tease" upon the heart, causing a painful yearning to rise up. It is a "wound" of love inflicted upon the heart, stirring up a longing for the infinite Mystery of God with the taste of an "I know not what" (*un no se que*) surpassing all understanding.[80]

The Eucharist is the narrow gate that opens us up to the great transcendent mystery of God's tremendous love. As the hidden spring of life, which we "know well" is tasted in prayer, the Eucharistic Lord can start stirring in us a certain holy affliction of languishing and thirsting for more of Him. This thirst, often arising in the empty aridity of the desert, is not to be avoided but rather cherished as drawing us deeper into the mystery of God. This holy anguish is a grace we must ask of the Lord. Wisdom-incarnate continues to speak to us from the Eucharistic Host: "Those who eat me will hunger for more, and those who drink me will thirst for more" (Sir. 24:21).

> *Let Us Pray:* Lord Jesus, please help me discover the vastness of Your presence in the Eucharist. Instill in me a tremendous awe and wonder. Please reveal and unfold the awesome mystery You are in the silence of my adoration. Help me find the hidden and vast spring of grace veiled in the Bread of Life, which satisfies while stirring up my hunger and thirst for more of You. St. John of the Cross, please pray for me. Amen.

[80] Ibid.

## Today's Reflection

*What caught your attention today in the writings
and lived witness of St. John of the Cross?*

*One tiny Host contains all the mysteries of the
universe: the living water, Bread from Heaven.
Which of these mysteries do you most long to fully
understand? Ask the Lord to illuminate your heart.*

Day 20

# St. Teresa of Calcutta (Mother Teresa): Contemplative Belonging

*Jesus Himself must be the one to say to you "I Thirst." Hear your own name. Not just once. Every day. If you listen with your heart, you will hear, you will understand. Why does Jesus say, "I thirst"? What does it mean? Something so hard to explain in words.... "I thirst" is something much deeper than just Jesus saying "I love you." Until you know deep inside that Jesus thirsts for you—you can't begin to know who He wants to be for you. Or who He wants you to be for Him.*

—Mother Teresa[81]

In our first eleven days we covered two great themes. First, the relationship between the hidden Christ in the Eucharist and the hidden Christ in others. Second, God's desire for our love. Today

---

[81] Mother Teresa, Letter to the Missionaries of Charity ("Varanasi Letter"), March 25, 1993, full text at St. Stephen Catholic Church, Bentonville.

we will revisit these themes under the guidance of St. Teresa of Calcutta (Mother Teresa).

We come to find the Lord in the round Host as the center-point of all reality. But we also find Him in the round Host as the great circumference of all reality. What do I mean? The Eucharist as center-point and circumference means that our times of returning to the center in Eucharistic Adoration radically effects our going out from the chapel to the circumference, the outer reaches of the spheres we inhabit. Our belonging to God encompasses our whole lives.

The twofold command of love of God and of neighbor (see Luke 10:27) has a Eucharistic dimension. Its center-point is in the love of God in the Eucharist, and its circumference is in all the varied encounters with our neighbors out in the world. St. Teresa of Calcutta lived this out in an exemplary way, her whole life focused on Jesus not just in the chapel but everywhere she went. Mother Teresa found Jesus hidden both in the Eucharist and in her neighbor. The mode of the presence of Christ is different in each. We genuflect toward the tabernacle, yet our neighbor too provides us with an encounter with Christ. "You did it to Me" — Mother liked to repeat this phrase as a five-word summary of the Gospel (see Matt. 25:40), in which Christ speaks about doing good "to the least of these" as doing good directly to him. "You did it to Me" summarized Mother Teresa's mission of love: to touch Christ in our neighbor.

Every human person is made in the image of God (Gen. 1:27). Each person, moreover, gives us a glimpse of Christ, who is the perfect image of God (Col. 1:15). All are meant "to be conformed to the image of his Son, in order that he might be the first-born among many brethren" (Rom. 8:29). The same faith that causes us to recognize Jesus hidden in the Eucharist causes us to recognize

Him in our neighbor. As we grow in one, we grow in the other. We go from adoring and finding Jesus in the Eucharist to contemplating and finding Him in our neighbor throughout the rest of our day until we return to Him in the Eucharist. St. Mother Teresa was like the bride of the Song of Songs, going through the streets looking for her beloved (3:3), looking for him in the distressing disguise of the poor. And it was the same faith that recognized Him under the appearance of ordinary bread in the Eucharist that recognized Him in the appearance of her neighbor. Center-point and circumference were encompassed by her Eucharistic faith.

This Eucharistic faith kept Mother Teresa searching for Christ everywhere, and it transformed her whole life. As handed on to the Missionaries of Charity, Mother Teresa sought a life that was "deeply contemplative, intensely Eucharistic, and vibrant with joy." For our belonging to the Lord to encompass our whole life, it too needs to be these three things. It must be "intensely Eucharistic" as the objective Real Presence of Jesus transforms all of space and time for us as we go forth and return to the Eucharist fervently as source and summit. It must be "deeply contemplative" as we look beyond superficial appearances to hidden realities and recognize the hidden presence of God wherever we find Him. And as a result of these two, it will surely be a life "vibrant with joy" as all is suffused with the gentle light of our divine Beloved.

What keeps this deeply contemplative seeking and finding of the Lord fervent is not so much our enkindled desire as it is the God who "is a consuming fire" (Heb. 12:29). "We love, because he first loved us" (1 John 4:19). On day 1 we noted that the *Catechism* says: "Whether we realize it or not, prayer is the encounter of God's thirst with ours. God thirsts that we may thirst for him" (no. 2560). On the wall of every Missionary of Charity chapel, one finds the words "I thirst!" (John 19:28). For them — and for us—it is crucial to believe in Jesus' personal thirst for each of us as a present, living reality.

Mother wrote to her sisters words about Jesus' thirst that we can take to heart as well: "It is very important for us to know that Jesus is thirsting for our love, for the love of the whole world.... Ask yourself. Have I heard Jesus directly say this word to me personally? Did I ever hear that word personally? 'I thirst.' 'I want your love.'... If not, examine yourself: Why could I not hear?"[82]

In a previous letter, she wrote:

> Jesus Himself must be the one to say to you "I Thirst." Hear you own name. Not just once. Every day. If you listen with your heart, you will hear, you will understand. Why does Jesus say, "I Thirst"? What does it mean? Something so hard to explain in words.... "I thirst" is something much deeper than just Jesus saying "I love you." Until you know deep inside that Jesus thirsts for you—you can't begin to know who He wants to be for you. Or who He wants you to be for Him.[83]

What is it that God wants to be for us? Our strong support and refuge. The one on whom we can cast ourselves in our desperation and poverty. What does God want us to be for Him? The one who abides close to Him, knowing himself to be loved and cherished by the Lord as we return love for love and so quench His thirst. To belong more fully to God, we need to receive in faith how much He truly wants to belong to us. Eucharistic Adoration is a

---

[82] St. Teresa of Calcutta, Letter to the Missionaries of Charity, December 1, 1983.

[83] St. Teresa of Calcutta, Letter to the Missionaries of Charity, March 25, 1993.

key setting to hear these words that Jesus speaks to us personally in the present moment: "I thirst!" His indefatigable thirst then becomes that strong bond that keeps us close to Him and Him close to us.

St. Mother Teresa invites us to reflect: "That word, 'I thirst,' has it penetrated into my heart? We are called to quench the thirst of God!"[84] When we receive it with a lively faith, that unflagging thirst of Jesus becomes the strong bond of our belonging to God and the driving force that draws us to His Eucharistic heart.

*Let Us Pray:* O Jesus, my heart is sometimes dry and weary. At times I feel disconnected from Your longing for me in the Eucharist. Please touch the dry and thirsting areas of my heart so I may know with conviction that You desire me with infinite desire and love. Help me to hear "I thirst" from Your Eucharistic heart. May this "thirst" awaken in me great longings for You and love for serving You in my neighbor.

## Today's Reflection

*"I thirst," Jesus whispered to Mother Teresa, just as he does to us. How will you quench the thirst of Jesus today?*

*How can your life, like Mother Teresa's, be more "deeply contemplative, intensely Eucharistic, and vibrant with joy"?*

---

[84] St. Teresa of Calcutta, Letter to the Missionaries of Charity, September 23, 1985.

Day 21

# St. Catherine of Siena: "Eyes Like a Flame of Fire"

*And we are put on earth a little space,*
*That we may learn to bear the beams of love.*

—William Blake[85]

St. Catherine of Siena envisions the Eucharist as a bright, burning Sun in our midst, blazing with an intensity beyond the sun in the sky. Ponder this as you come before our Eucharistic Lord in the chapel. It is a bit of a miracle that you are not scorched and burned up coming so close to the divine Sun. It is the gift of the veil of faith in this life that William Blake's words above so eloquently capture. The God of all majesty became a little baby and a little Host for us, that we might draw near to Him and grow in intimate love of Him through the veil of faith before He is manifested in full splendor in Heaven and we are blessedly consumed by those blazing beams of love for all eternity.

[85] "The Little Black Boy," Poetry.com, https://www.poetry.com/poem/39180/the-little-black-boy.

God is a blazing fire for St. Catherine. It is not hard therefore to understand why she resorts to the image of the sun to describe the Trinity. She sees the sun's brightness as a metaphor for the Father, while the sun's color suggests something of the Son, and the sun's heat corresponds to the Holy Spirit. Like all images of the Trinity, the image is limited and inexact, but St. Catherine uses it to grapple with the mystery of God as three-in-one. God draws close to us in Jesus and the Eucharist so that we now have the bright, shining sun blazing forth in the chapel with us. Catherine hears God the Father say of Jesus, "His body is indeed a sun, for it is one thing with me, the true Sun."[86]

In contemplative prayer in the presence of the Eucharist, we open our souls to the sun like spring flowers to receive life, light, and the warmth of love from this sun. Catherine hears from God that we ourselves then take on the qualities of the sun: "I told you that those who were perfect took on the qualities of the sun. They gave the light and warmth of loving charity to their neighbors, and because of this warmth they bore fruit and caused virtue to spring up in the souls of their subjects."[87] We come into the presence of the Sun, soaking in God's rays of love, and we leave the chapel, as is commonly said, sunburned. Drawing close to the Sun, we are also made bright, full of light, and burning with charity.

The Sienese saint sees in the Eucharistic heart of Jesus a most sublime glory. A few days ago we explored the gaze of Jesus on us with St. Manuel. St. Catherine helps us, however, develop an awareness of the potential of our own gaze. How do we best gaze upon the Lord in the Eucharist? St. Catherine guides us forward. Catherine says in a letter, "Contemplate the truth in the abyss of

---

[86] St. Catherine of Siena, *The Dialogue*, no. 110.
[87] Ibid., no. 120.

divine charity."[88] Try to see everything more in the light of God's love. Over time we can come to see God's love smiling through all things. We grow in this as we gaze upon our Eucharistic Lord. Catherine gives this a more personalist tenor in another letter: "Gaze into the eye of the divine charity with which God looked on his creatures before he created us. And so He still looks on us.... I want you to be engulfed and set on fire in Him, constantly gazing into the gentle eye of His charity, for then you will love what He loves, and hate what he hates."[89]

We gaze into the eye of divine charity precisely as we gaze with faith upon the person of Jesus in the Eucharist. We look into the eyes of our Lord, and we see His love burning for us and for others. These are the eyes of Jesus that John the Beloved gazed into and described as "like a flame of fire" (Rev. 1:14). And these are the same eyes we get to gaze into as we perceive the personal presence of Jesus in the Eucharist. Gazing into the gentle eye of His charity, we will begin to see and love like He does. The Eucharist is like a blazing sun, an immense fire of love, not simply as an abstract reality but as the personal presence of Jesus with His gaze full of a personal love for us.

It is as if God continues to plead with us through St. Catherine: "O dearest daughter, open wide your mind's eye and look into the abyss of my charity. There is not a person whose heart would not melt in love to see, among all the other blessings I have given you, the blessing you receive in this sacrament. And how, dearest daughter, should you and others look upon this mystery and touch it?"[90] Catherine is introducing us here to what we could

---

[88] St. Catherine of Siena, *The Letters of Catherine of Siena*, T46.
[89] Ibid., T204.
[90] *Dialogue*, no. 111.

call a spirituality of the Eucharistic gaze. How do we do it? What is it like to gaze into the eyes of Jesus in the Eucharist, into the eyes of divine love?

Catherine notes that with our bodily eyes we just see simple bread, but the eyes of faith look more deeply and perceive the living Lord, true God and true man. The soul develops a sort of instinct of faith, a sensitivity of soul through the perception of faith and connaturality of charity. It is worth quoting St. Catherine at length in her own words:

> What tastes and sees and touches this sacrament? The soul's sensitivity. How does she see it? With her mind's eye, so long as it has the pupil of holy faith.... How is this sacrament touched? With the hand of love.... The hand of love touches through faith, confirming as it were what the soul sees and knows spiritually through faith. How is this sacrament tasted? With holy desire. The body tastes only the flavor of bread, but the soul tastes me, God and human.... So you see, you must receive this sacrament not only with your bodily senses but with your spiritual sensitivity, by disposing your soul to see and receive and taste this sacrament with affectionate love.[91]

We dispose our souls to see and taste the Lord with faith and affectionate love through our habitual practice of adoration. We cultivate all this through recognizing the personal presence of Jesus in the Eucharist, speaking to Him as a friend and listening in silence. Yes, God is a deep Sea of Love, a blazing Sun of Fire, but He is these things as the personal God. We gaze at Him who gazes at us. His eyes are like a flame of fire (Rev. 1:14). As one

---

[91] Ibid.

might lose himself in the eyes of a beloved, so we lose ourselves gazing into the Sacrament of Love and the gentle eye of divine charity. Our eyes too can become aflame with fire.

*Let Us Pray:* O God, You are a consuming fire! Stir up in me the desire to draw forth from Your Eucharistic heart all the graces I need to grow in holiness. Help me gaze on You with greater devotion and perception. Help us to discover in Your Eucharistic gaze a sea of love and peace. Enlighten me, Lord, to look into the depths of Your heart. With a simple gaze of love, let me be so fascinated by You to be drawn out of myself into a life completely lived for You and others.

## Today's Reflection

*Was there a particular line or idea from the writings
of St. Catherine that caught your attention?*

*Do you see the Eucharist "with the pupils of holy faith"?
How is this different from looking with physical eyes?*

Day 22

# John Tauler: Consuming and Being Consumed

*When we consume this Food, we ourselves are being consumed.*

—St. Bernard of Clairvaux[92]

We are aware of the wonderful marvel involved in receiving Jesus in the Eucharist. Yet have we realized that, as we consume Him, we ourselves are being consumed by the Lord? St. Bernard of Clairvaux was perhaps the first writer to make this surprising reversal to our common way of thinking in his commentary on the *Song of Songs*, but others follow after him, from Bl. John Ruusbroec to St. Elizabeth of the Trinity. The fourteenth-century Dominican John Tauler also ponders the Eucharist in terms of our being consumed by the Lord in his first two sermons for *Corpus Christi*. We will ponder the mystery with him. While he is not a canonized saint, he is considered one of the greatest mystics and preachers of the Middle Ages, being both sublime and practical.

---

[92] St. Bernard of Clairvaux, *Commentary on the Song of Songs*, no. 71.5.

St. Augustine famously observed that with ordinary food, the food is turned into us, but in the Eucharist, it is we who are turned into what we receive, Jesus Christ.[93] The later language of the mystics about being consumed by the Lord in Eucharistic Communion builds on this. It examines more precisely what needs to be consumed in us for our transformation in Christ to be complete. From our sinfulness to our self-centeredness, much has to be consumed to be able to truly say with St. Paul, "I have been crucified with Christ; it is no longer I who live, but Christ who lives in me" (Gal. 2:20). This is what Eucharistic Communion is to bring us to in becoming totally His.

John Tauler, building on Augustine and Bernard, ponders how we ourselves are consumed through Eucharistic Communion and a Eucharistic life of self-giving. How are we consumed? To begin with, by painful self-knowledge and compunction for our sinful tendencies. Then, through the trials and afflictions that make up God's plan for us, as ordered to our purification and death to self, that Christ may live fully in us. John Tauler notes, "God feasts upon us; as He enters He scourges us for our sins, which He reveals plainly to us—His divine presence scourges our conscience.... Dear child, gladly endure this biting of God's presence in thee, let Him eat thee and chew thee to pieces."[94] While Tauler recognizes that God's gentle love is behind this all, he chooses to

---

93  See St. Augustine, "Augustine on the Nature of the Sacrament of the Eucharist," Sermon 272, Early Church Texts, https://www.earlychurchtexts.com/public/augustine_sermon_272_eucharist.htm.

94  John Tauler, "On Holy Communion—First Sermon for the Feast of Corpus Christi," in *The Sermons and Conferences of John Tauler of the Order of Preachers*, trans. Walter Elliott (Apostolic Mission House, 1910), 370.

use this graphic language to capture what we sometimes feel in the midst of trials or when we see ugly parts of ourselves in light of the All-Holy One. It rings true to experience.

A little later, Tauler, as he ponders the hard trials that can afflict us, speaks of God hunting us as a hunter and wanting to consume us as His prey. God uses human beings as hunting dogs to pursue us and tear apart those prideful aspects of us that often come to the fore in our human relationships.

> Herein does a man find himself hunted like a wild animal that the emperor's huntsmen pursue, in order that their master can capture him.... Now the heavenly Father has His hunting hounds everywhere — in convents and monasteries; in our homes and in cities, and in the forests; and you may be certain that all chosen friends of God are going to be sorely hunted by all created things. As the hart is driven by the hunters, tormented with thirst, so must thou be driven on till thou findest thy refuge in God.[95]

Trials and an undying thirst force us to find our refuge in God alone as everything else fails us. Tauler's language is somewhat cruel and brutal because this is how the events and afflictions of life can feel. Tauler wants to be honest about the difficulty while helping us see that it is God who is at work in what can seem so harsh. It is by being consumed as God's prey, and chewed up, that nothing of our old self remains and we can be transformed into a new man or woman in Jesus Christ. Food that is chewed up can be transformed into something higher than what it was, as it is

---

[95] John Tauler, "Dispositions for Holy Communion — Second Sermon for the Feast of Corpus Christi," in *Sermons and Conferences*, 376.

absorbed into the human body. A similar absorption happens in consuming the Eucharist, but it is we who are transformed into something higher.

As the old self and self-centered inclinations are chewed up through trials to which we surrender in love, we are absorbed into God, into a deeper participation in the divine nature (see 2 Pet. 1:4). What is called for here is our trust. Tauler explains, "After the chastisement comes a gentle softening of one's soul, loving trust, divine confidence, holy hope: it is now that God is absorbing and, as it were, swallowing thee.... But thou must give thyself up to our Lord with all trust, and then shalt thou be gently absorbed in Him."[96] Trustful and loving surrender to the Lord is key in allowing ourselves to be consumed and more fully transformed by these God-ordained trials in our lives.

We consume the Lord in the Eucharist, but the Lord also consumes us. Perhaps we discover something of a rhythm between these two realities in the back-and-forth between Holy Communion and Eucharistic Adoration. In receiving Holy Communion at Mass, it makes sense that we would focus on the one we are receiving into our hearts as we consume the Sacred Host. Eucharistic Adoration, on the other hand, may be the more fitting time to perceive in faith how the Lord is consuming us through the particular trials and afflictions of our life. We can offer ourselves in loving and trustful surrender with the Sacred Host as we are being consumed by the Lord and are being consumed as a living holocaust. How often we leave the Eucharistic Adoration chapel with a different and more faith-filled perspective on life than when we entered! When we come to see these afflictions as chewing away at our old self so we can be remade more fully in Christ,

---

[96] Tauler, "On Holy Communion," 370.

then we can, like Mother Teresa of Calcutta, love the Lord not so much for what He gives but for what He takes. The latter is transforming us into a holocaust wholly consumed. It is God's beloved prey being consumed by Him.

John Tauler helps us discern how things are proceeding here and holds before our eyes the goal for which we strive. "Thou shalt find out if thou art absorbed into God as His food, if thou are so changed as to find nothing in thyself except Him, and findest thyself nowhere else but in Him.... This adorable Sacrament separates all that is bad, profitless and superfluous, casting it all out of the soul; and then God enters into all one's life, love, thought, intention, making all newer, cleaner and more divine."[97]

> *Let Us Pray:* Lord, I thank You for the gift of receiving and even consuming You in the Eucharist. Grant me the grace to be as thankful for the ways You consume me in our Eucharistic life together. Devour me, Lord, in Your love. I want to be consumed by You. Absorb me ever more into Your life. Transform me into Yourself. I long to be one with You. Totally Yours. As I kneel before Your Eucharistic Presence offered to the Father with such love, help me to offer myself with You completely in trust, surrender, and love. Amen.

[97] Ibid., 371.

## Today's Reflection

*What idea—perhaps from the writings of John Tauler—stayed with you as you read?*

*As we consume the Eucharist, we are consumed, purified, and transformed. Have you experienced this? If not, invite Jesus to do this work in you.*

## Part III

# Praying with Scripture

These final eleven days we will spend musing on the Word of God with Fr. Ignatius John Schweitzer, O.P. What follows is not so much a historical critical study of the Sacred Scriptures nor a systematic scriptural exegesis as such. These coming days are more about praying with Scripture and at times exploring the different senses or layers of the inexhaustible Word of God to better catch a glimpse of the mystery of the Eucharist (cf. CCC 112–118).

In a certain sense, we have already drunk from the Word in the contagious Eucharistic spirituality of the saints. The lives and words of the saints are in many ways icons of the Word of God. By embodying the gospel in their lives, the saints help us interpret Sacred Scripture. Having said this, while the saints live the Word, we want to drink more deeply at the font of revelation explicitly. We want to feast on the Scriptures in this section.

Brothers and sisters, you are in for a treat because the Word of God is full of light. Its mystical radiance can truly ignite our hearts in profound ways. It puts us directly in touch with the sacred mysteries of God and God Himself.

These days ahead are overflowing with the light of the Word. May pondering these mysteries in these last days toward consecration deeply imprint a burning love for our Eucharistic Lord upon our hearts.

Day 23

# Elijah and Eucharistic Contemplation

*"Arise and eat, else the journey will be too great
for you." And [Elijah] arose, and ate and drank,
and went in the strength of that food forty days
and forty nights to Horeb the mount of God.*

—1 Kings 19:7–8

We begin with the ever-living charism of Elijah as a model for our Eucharistic life. Elijah stands out of the sacred page almost as an ideal. He is chosen as representative of the prophets at the Transfiguration of Christ, appearing with Moses the Lawgiver (Matt. 17:1–8). Moreover, in both the Old and New Testaments, he is seen as the prophet connected to preparing for the most significant event of all, the eschatological Day of the Lord at the end of time (Mal. 4:5–6; Matt. 17:10–13).

Why is Elijah seen as such an ideal prophet? He brings together in one figure (1) the heights of the contemplative life, (2) the anointed prophetic word, and (3) the establishing of right worship. And so, strengthened by mysterious bread for his journey

(1 Kings 19:7–8), Elijah shines as an ideal for our Eucharistic life of (1) contemplation, (2) preaching, and (3) worship.

First, in Elijah we find a contemplative who stands steadfast before the Lord on the mountaintop in prayer, even amidst the storms of prayer. He responds to the Lord's beckoning: " 'Go out and stand on the mount before the Lord.' And behold, the Lord passed by, and a great and strong wind tore the mountains and broke in pieces the rocks before the Lord" (1 Kings 19:11, ESV). At times, as the worn and wearied contemplative, Elijah can only muster enough strength to simply abide before the Lord: "Elijah went up to the top of Mount Carmel. And he bowed himself down on the earth and put his face between his knees" (18:42, ESV). As the story is picked up in 2 Kings, Elijah is found again in prayer raised aloft, "sitting on the top of a hill." There he is addressed as "O man of God," and, as a true man of God, he speaks a powerful word and calls down fire from Heaven, precisely as he abides before the Lord steadfastly (2 Kings 1:9-10).

Elijah's prophetic word is so powerful precisely because he stands firm before the Lord. His hidden life is foundational. In the beginning of his vocation, "the word of the Lord came to him: 'Depart from here and turn eastward and hide yourself by the brook Cherith" (1 Kings 17:2–3). Notice that the first word received by Elijah is *"hide yourself* by the brook Cherith." This is the first call of all of us: to cultivate the hidden life before the face of the Eucharistic Lord.

It is interesting to note that the word *Cherith* means "cutting away." For the hidden, contemplative life of the desert, whether the literal desert or the arid space of the Eucharistic Adoration chapel, is an empty space where things are "cut away." Unhelpful attachments, other people's opinions, worldly thinking, and egotism are quietly cut away in this space of prayer, and we stand naked before the Lord. It is the mountain of God, whether Mount Horeb or Mount Carmel or an adoration chapel on top of a little hill—a space where all else is "cut away" and God alone dwells. It is then that the Lord is encountered in that "still[,] small voice" that, while hardly noticed, shakes our world to the core (1 Kings 19:12). And it is only in that still, small voice of the Lord that our voices come to thunder as we peacefully speak God's Word to the world.

Second, through his prayer, Elijah's preaching powerfully cuts to the heart. Elijah enters the narrative of the Bible with no introduction. Abruptly, without indicating his family line, the first line about him indicates that he stands before the living God in prayer and speaks a prophetic word from this place of prayer. This is simply who he is and captures his whole identity. "Now Eli'jah the Tishbite, of Tishbe in Gilead, said to Ahab, 'As the Lord, the God of Israel, lives, *before whom I stand*, there shall be neither dew nor rain these years, except by my word'" (1 Kings 17:1, emphasis added). As a model for us, Elijah speaks while standing rooted in the mystery of God, with "the hand of the Lord" upon him (18:46), and so his words ring forth with a divine depth. It is not his own word but the word *of God* he speaks, a word properly received and spoken only in the presence of God.

I recall a preacher who began to make a daily Eucharistic holy hour. It was not too long until the religious sisters to whom he regularly preached began to bear witness to the new depth from which he spoke. Like Elijah, we too can proclaim "the God who answers by fire, he is God" (18:24). When we ponder the Scriptures before our Eucharistic Lord, he brings us into contact with his fiery word of power and our words bear something more of the divine in them. We bear witness, not by preaching the Gospel with our words, but with our very lives that reveal the presence of the living God who dwells in us and speaks through us as we arise from Eucharistic Adoration with the fire of Eljah (see Sir. 48:1).

Third, Elijah, whose name means "The Lord is my God," embodies in his very person the mission of drawing others into right whole-hearted worship: "The Lord, he is God; the Lord, he is God" (1 Kings 18:39). Elijah unveils the emptiness of false gods, but more importantly he draws people to the true and living God, making of their worship a fragrant offering to God. "Then Eli'jah said to all the people, 'Come near to me'; and all the people came near to him. And he repaired the altar of the Lord" (18:30). In our building a culture of right worship through the Mass and Eucharistic Adoration, we follow Elijah's lead and invite people to "Come near," or more exactly, "Come along with me to worship our Eucharistic Lord"—"Come and see" (John 1:39). Our words can influence how others worship, but even more powerful than this is drawing others into worship with us in an atmosphere of reverence, devotion, and love. Our call is to build a culture of worship, "for glory and for beauty" (Exod. 28:2), where God is placed on the throne and His children find freedom and purpose under the "bright cloud" of His presence (see Matt. 17:5).

Elijah rebuilds the altar with twelve stones, after the twelve tribes of *Israel* (1 Kings 18:31–32). Israel means "God prevails." God prevails over all else. Sometimes, putting God first in worship and exalting Him above all else feels like a risk. We often have to pay the cost of extolling God above all else. We pay the cost with our time, energy, priorities, money, and our knees. But God prevails here too. He continues to give the word and speak the name *Israel* over our altars of self-offering, for He will continue to prevail over all we risk for His sake. In Elijah's call of the prophet Elisha, Elisha sacrificed his very livelihood: "plowing with twelve yoke of oxen," he "took the yoke of oxen and sacrificed them"

(19:19, 21, ESV). And in following a more radical way of the Lord, he did not look back.

We have followed Elijah's threefold charism in light of the Eucharist: (1) to live a hidden, contemplative life before the Eucharistic face of our Lord; (2) to share an anointed word of the Lord that has the Eucharist as its source; and (3) to draw others into an intensely Eucharistic life of adoration and worship of God. Only with the Eucharist will we be able to say with Elijah, "I have been very zealous for the Lord" (1 Kings, 19:10, 14, NRSVCE). Only with the Eucharist will we be able to call down fire and be taken up in the chariots of fire of contemplation. May the Lord give us this threefold *Elijah-grace* so that we may hasten His Second Coming through our Eucharistic contemplation, preaching, and worship. For He has promised, "Behold, I will send you Elijah the prophet before the great and awesome day of the Lord comes" (Mal. 4:5, ESV).

*Let Us Pray:* Heavenly Father, draw me to Your Son and hide me in His heart where that stream of living water flows. Help me bear a divine word of life to the world. Use me to draw others to worship and adore You, and help me be a witness of right reverence and ardent love. May I be part of the renewal of worship in Your Church, for You alone are Lord. Amen.

## Today's Reflection

*Was there a particular line or idea that stood out to you in today's reflection?*

*How does the hidden, contemplative life prepare us for the "Day of the Lord"?*

Day 24

# Mary Magdalene: Pressing into Jesus

*Faith reaches what is unreachable, makes known
what is unknown, grasps what cannot be measured,
plumbs the uttermost depths, and in a way encompasses
even eternity itself in its wide embrace.*

—St. Bernard of Clairvaux[98]

"The crowd was pressing in on Jesus and listening to the word of God" (Luke 5:1, NABRE). This is precisely what we do in Eucharistic Adoration. We press in on Jesus and listen to the Word of God as we ponder the Scriptures. The same Greek word for "pressing" (*epikeimai*) appears in Mark 3:10, "all who had diseases pressed upon Him to touch Him." This Gospel scene is part of the picture for us too in Eucharistic Adoration. We come with our utter need and press in on Jesus, leaning into Him and His love with all our hearts. As our mind's eye,

---

[98] St. Bernard of Clairvaux, *Commentary on the Song of Songs*, no. 76.6. All notes in this reflection are keyed to this work.

intention, and loving focus is directed outside of ourselves to the Lord, we press in on Him, and penetrate more deeply into His mysterious presence, love, and salvation. We cast ourselves on the Lord with all the weight of our need and desperation and, tumbling toward Him, we come to find ourselves in the same position of the beloved disciple, leaning on the heart of Jesus with all the weight of our love.

In a way, St. Mary Magdalene prefigures all adorers of our Eucharistic Lord, as she abides, remaining at the Cross and remaining by the tomb, longing for the Lord, even after all the others have gone away to do something else. Surely if she were alive in our own day, she would be one of those holy souls who linger before the tabernacle after Mass or abide in the Eucharistic Adoration chapel as if in a home, their true home before the Lord. And at the tomb, now made empty, she presses more deeply into the mystery of Christ: "as she wept she stooped to look into the tomb" (John 20:11). It is as if that open, spacious tomb mirrors the open spaciousness of her faith, ready to receive the ever-greater mystery that the Lord wishes to lead her into.

St. Bernard of Clairvaux describes the Magdalene's faith in terms of her encounter with the Risen Christ, who says to her: "Don't cling to me" (John 20:17, NLT). He says this only because he wishes to initiate her beyond the mere physical touch into a more substantial touch through faith, hope, and charity. St. Bernard writes:

> Learn to receive with greater confidence, to follow with greater security, whatever faith commends to you. "Do not touch me, for I have not yet ascended to my Father." ... And yet he could be touched, but by the heart, not by the hand; by desire, not by the eye; by faith, not by the senses....

In its deep and mystical breast, faith can grasp what is the length and breadth and height and depth. "You will touch me with the hand of faith, the finger of desire, the embrace of love." (no. 28.9–10)

St. Bernard places on the Lord's lips this promise of touching with faith, hope, and love, and we do this all the more as we press in on Jesus before Him in the Eucharist, as His presence radiates out, enfolds us, and possesses us.

Immersed in the mysterious presence of our Eucharistic Lord, we hear anew from His heart, "Put out into the deep" (Luke 5:4). We press into the immense deep sea of God's love and are beckoned to go even deeper. At times it is like what Bl. John Ruusbroec describes as a "rich wandering in super-essential Love," losing our own way in an enriching, self-transcending wandering as we enter beyond our ways more fully into the Way, the Truth, the Life. At other times, the experience of going deeper is like what is described by St. Luke, who tells of Jesus pushing off from the shore and teaching in a boat at a distance (Luke 5:3). Or like St. Peter, who reverently recognizes his own sinful self at a distance from the holy and exalted One (5:8). We seek to press in on the Lord and the Lord seems to keep us at a distance, inviting us to press forward into Him even more. We then have to listen to the teaching of Jesus from a felt distance. "Pressing in on Jesus and listening to the word of God" (Luke 5:1, NABRE). At such times the accent is on listening to His word even as our felt sense of His presence recedes and we are called to go out into the deep, more into the objective reality and truth of God, more apprehended by faith than our subjective experience of it.

William of St. Thierry, best friend of St. Bernard, counsels us, "Take refuge in the comfort of the Scriptures when deprived of the grace of spiritual consolation." The Scriptures are inherently comforting as they make known the objective reality of God and His plan for us. A time of dryness and aridity is a suitable time to feast on the objectively nourishing meal of Sacred Scripture. It is what Bernard calls "the sweet and wholesome spiritual feast of Sacred Scripture" (no. 73.2). Whether you take pleasure in a meal or not, it still nourishes you! Whether you feel God's presence or not, the Sacred Scriptures still bring you into contact with the mystery of God. The inspired Word of God mediates reality to us, and faith, hope, and charity reach out, touch, and press into the mystery. Bernard states it in all simplicity: "Believe, and you have found Him" (no. 76.6).

"Put out into the deep and let down your nets for a catch.... Do not be afraid; henceforth you will be catching men" (Luke 5:4, 10). As we press in on Jesus and listen to the Word of God in the adoration chapel, we do so also for our brothers and sisters. As the Lord draws us "with the bands of love" (Hos. 11:4), the spiritual bonds of affection we have for others draw them along with us too.

But we are also sent. Outside the adoration chapel, Jesus remains with us spiritually as we follow Him, in the poverty of leaving everything, even ourselves. And with the demands of the apostolic life stretching us and expanding our hearts, "always speaking to God and about God" (St. Dominic), who knows, at times, whether the "pressing in on Jesus and listening to the word of God" is the more profound in those times of active service? Contemplation to action, like those waves of the Sea of Love washing onto the shore. Action to contemplation, like those waves of love bringing back with them rich treasures gained along the journey and offered and pressed into the heart of God.

*Let Us Pray:* Lord, keep drawing me so I keep moving out into the deep through my times of Eucharistic Adoration and times of active service. Help me to reach out in faith and hope when things are other than I think they ought to be. In this way, draw me deeper into selfless charity, lost to self as I plunge deeper into You.

## Today's Reflection

*What drew your attention in today's reflection?*

*Ask the Lord to show you how you, like Mary Magdalene, can make yourself more "at home" with Jesus, "pressing in" to His presence.*

Day 25

# Emmanuel: God
# with Us, Now

*Lo, I am with you always,
to the close of the age.*

—Matthew 28:20

This side of eternity, when has God been most with us? In His Incarnation, or at His birth, or during His earthly ministry? I suggest that it is none of these things. The Incarnation is certainly the definite revelation of God, and so we will always return to the Gospels to behold the glory of God become man. However, there are good reasons for viewing the Age of the Church as the time that God has most been with us. And if this is the case, we have no reason to be envious of the first disciples or first generation of Christians. We have rather to claim by faith the great mystery we have now: Emmanuel, God with us, *now*.

During His earthly life, Jesus was confined to one geographic location. He could be in only one place at a time, whether in Bethlehem or Nazareth or walking the streets of Galilee. Back then, one might be so fortunate to draw so near to Jesus as to be just a couple feet away. Yet, consider the closeness of encounter with God we get to enjoy in our own day. We do not just get to approach within a couple feet of Him; we get to receive Him into our own bodies in the Eucharist. "Abide in me as I abide in you" (John 15:4, NRSVCE). In the Eucharist, we enjoy Emmanuel, God with us, in a way that surpasses the nearness of the first Christians. The Age of the Church is actually the high point of Emmanuel with us in this pilgrimage of faith.

Remember the words of the Lord: "I tell you the truth: it is to your advantage that I go away, for if I do not go away, the Counselor will not come to you" (John 16:7). Imagine being there with the apostles as Jesus speaks these surprising words. *How is that so, Lord? Really, is it better that You go away?!* Reactions like this, as understandable as they are, reveal that they have not yet realized the purpose of the Holy Spirit in the lives of believers, then and now. Two thousand years ago, we could have witnessed the events of Christ's life. We could have gazed upon the Cross from a distance or even close-up; and, like many of those bystanders, the true spiritual significance of the scene would have been lost on us. But after the Paschal Mystery and sending of the Holy Spirit, all the mysteries of Christ are accessible to us with an interior saving power and contact that transforms us.

In the Gospel of John, Jesus tells his first disciples that they already know the Holy Spirit through knowing Him, Jesus: "You know him, for he dwells with you, and will be in you" (John 14:17). The Spirit will be in us. This is the new thing that happens at Pentecost and in the Age of the Church. The Spirit brings to us the mysteries of Christ in a way that applies their salvific effect within us in a much more powerful way. St. Gregory of Nazianzus, caught up in the mystery of the Incarnation, exclaimed, "What is this mystery that is around me?!"[99] We are caught up in the mystery of Christ. We do not just gaze upon the events of Christ's life, like many of His contemporaries did, without being changed. Rather, God is with us and transforming us from the inside out through His Spirit within us.

We might also envy the first disciples for being able to hear Jesus speak and teach. Yet many of Jesus' contemporaries listened to Him without it changing them. Jesus continues to speak to us too through the inspired Word of God. And the Holy Spirit takes this universal message of the Scriptures and applies it to us personally. The Holy Spirit highlights what God wants to speak to each person today. Jesus says, "The Counselor, the Holy Spirit, whom the Father will send in my name, he will teach you all things and bring to your remembrance all that I have said to you" (John 14:26). This is an anointed, holy remembrance that the Spirit effects in us, a sacred remembering (*anamnesis*) that brings us into contact with the saving mysteries communicated through the Scriptures. The Word comes to us now with greater conviction and power through the working of the Holy Spirit. The man Jesus spoke in human words two thousand years ago, and the divine Word continues to speak to us in human words today through a prayerful pondering of the Bible.

It is to our advantage that we live in the Age of the Church, where God is with us in a way that is more intimate than any other age or dispensation—closer, in fact, to the way He will be with us in eternity in Heaven. In John 14:1–3, Jesus describes Heaven as the Father's house with many rooms or dwelling places. The image suggests something without exhausting what Heaven will

---

[99] St. Gregory of Nazianzus, "Oration 38: On the Theophany" in *New Advent* (newadvent.org/fathers/310238.htm).

be like. "In my Father's house are many rooms" suggests familiar intimacy. In Heaven, we will not be lost in the crowd. Yes, among the multitudes, there will surely be a blessed self-forgetfulness as we are caught up in adoration among the masses, yet we will not just be a number. We will dwell in familiar intimacy with the Lord. You know personally those with whom you share a room, as together you experience the warmth of divine intimacy. In the Age of the Church, the many rooms of the Father's house seem to be prefigured by Eucharistic Adoration chapels or communities gathering around the Eucharist. There is familiar intimacy enjoyed by each one around the tabernacle, and yet there are many tabernacles spread throughout the world, like the many rooms in the Father's house.

The way Jesus operates in the Age of the Church also suggests something of how we will hear Jesus in Heaven. The same public revelation found in the Bible is offered to all, yet through the Holy Spirit it is personalized to each person. Jesus continues to speak to us today. He speaks interiorly. This seems to point us in the right direction for pondering how Jesus will speak to each of us in Heaven. He will not only be addressing millions as at a rally but will also be speaking interiorly to each one, with unique particular words of love for each individual through the working of the Holy Spirit. The words will certainly be clearer then but will seemingly come, at least in part, interiorly. The time we spend in the Eucharistic Adoration chapel, the Bible open on our lap and listening interiorly to Jesus, is getting us ready for Heaven. Something of the veiled quality of the sacraments and Scriptures will pass away, no doubt, but praying with the Word and Eucharist are the best preparations for "What no eye has seen, nor ear heard, nor the heart of man conceived, what God has prepared for those who love him" (1 Cor. 2:9).

The Wedding Feast of the Lamb ultimately belongs to eternity, but we get a foretaste of it even now in the Age of the Church as God dwells with us as Emmanuel, our Eucharistic Lord with us and in us.

*Let Us Pray:* Lord, awaken my faith to recognize how intimately You dwell with me as Emmanuel in the Eucharist and the Word of God. Presence, word, action—these things make up a human relationship, and so I enjoy this human relationship with You now. Help me reach forward to that day where You will be all in all. Amen.

## Today's Reflection

*What struck you in a fresh or unique way about
the role of the Holy Spirit in our lives?*

*Adoration is an ongoing exchange of love, a conversation
between Lover and beloved. Go to adoration and
listen intently as you read from your Bible. What do
you sense the Lord saying to you in particular?*

# I AM: Ultimate Reality

*I am He, the One speaking to you*
*(Ego eimi, ho lalon soi).*

—John 4:26, NASB

All reality finds its center-point in Jesus. Jesus is true God. Jesus is also true man, the high point of all creation. He is the one mediator between God and man, He is our oneness with God. He not only saves us, He *is* salvation. He is our all, and He comes to us and abides with us . . . in the Eucharist.

Whatever we are experiencing or not experiencing, whatever our subjective state, this is the objective truth. In Eucharistic Adoration, we come before this reality and cling to it, cling to Him in faith. All darkness, emptiness, and voids do not matter here. He is the All. Ponder this ancient text anew in the Lord's Eucharistic presence.

> He is the image of the invisible God,
> the firstborn of all creation.
> For by him all things were created, in heaven and on earth,
> visible and invisible,

whether thrones or dominions or rulers or authorities —
all things were created through him and for him.
And he is before all things,
and in him all things hold together.
And he is the head of the body, the church.
He is the beginning, the firstborn from the dead,
that in everything he might be preeminent.
For in him all the fullness of God was pleased to dwell,
and through him to reconcile to himself all things,
whether on earth or in heaven, making peace by the blood
    of his cross. (Col. 1:15–20, ESV)

All this is before us in the Eucharist. He is before us. Let the immensity of this reality strike you. Sleep no longer. Be awake to His living presence, true God and true man, the Mediator, the Savior, our salvation. All our efforts and interior dispositions, however important, take a second place. "These are only a shadow of what is to come, but the substance belongs to Christ" (Col. 2:17).

Whatever you are going through in life, take some moments to let these things take second place to Him, enthroned on the altar. Allow Him to be enthroned once again on the altar of your heart. Do this and all else will submit and bow before His feet. The difficulties, struggles, anxieties, doubt, and indifference will bow down before His feet and name Him Lord. With the Lord Jesus at the center of your life once again, everything else will fall into its proper place, ordered to Him.

Do you lack peace? "He Himself is our peace" (Eph. 2:14, NASB). He is the reconciliation of man and God. Come back and rest on Him, He who bridges earth to Heaven, man to God. "He Himself is our peace." Stop trying to find peace in yourself. Find it in Him! "He Himself is our peace." Let that reality soak in. It is already accomplished. St. Gregory of Nyssa prays, "In you, O Word of God our soul finds its still-point." Peace, not necessarily in the exterior circumstances or even in our conscious state, but in Him. "He Himself is our peace."

What is more important? Your experience or the objective reality before you in the Eucharist? What is more important? Your doubts and uncertainties or He who says, "I am … the truth" (John 14:6)? What is more important? Your changing feelings or this stable and weighty reality of the One who simply says, "I AM!"? Choose the Lord over yourself. Receive this reality in faith. Do not try to produce a feeling but rather simply acknowledge the reality in faith. No matter what you feel or do not feel, receive the Lord Jesus in faith. It is a simple act we can choose to make: "I believe, Lord, that you are present." "I believe that you, Jesus, are in charge as Lord." "I believe that every promise and word you speak is true … more true than me!" Let that act of faith become a constant stance, a simple acknowledgment of the truth. He is present. It is the Lord. Your feelings or awareness do not make Him present. He IS. He is present and loves you. He is accomplishing His good and beautiful plan for you. Let go and accept this with a simple faith: "Yes, I believe."

"Therefore, as you received Christ Jesus the Lord, so walk in him, rooted and built up in him and established in the faith, just as you were taught, abounding in thanksgiving" (Col. 2:6–7, ESV). Even as we leave the chapel, we remain rooted in the truth. God remains our foundation. Walk by faith. Do not expect to walk by sight or by feeling. Simply acknowledge the truth of God with acts of faith, little prayers whispered to God throughout your day. Surround faith with its proper atmosphere and it will flourish: Live by faith "abounding in thanksgiving" (Col. 2:7). Thanks and praise are the proper atmosphere of faith in God.

Like rising incense, in the chapel and out of the chapel, let praise and thanks arise and you will walk and even soar in the things of faith. Faith simply acknowledges the truth that God has revealed. "Be thankful. Let the word of Christ dwell in you richly, teaching and admonishing one another in all wisdom, singing psalms and hymns and spiritual songs, with thankfulness in your hearts to God" (Col. 3:15–16, ESV).

How marvelous is this reality we perceive through faith! Jesus is at the center. In Him is "every spiritual blessing in the heavenly places" (Eph. 1:3), "all the treasures of wisdom and knowledge" (Col. 2:3). Perceiving this, our hearts are elevated in praise and thanks. Moreover, lifting our hearts in praise and thanks helps us perceive this objective reality more fully. We intuitively know that we are thankful only for that which is ours. Hence, being thankful for our salvation, even when we do not see it, expands our experience of salvation. We are thankful when we have received something, so gratitude stirs up our faith in the invisible things we have received. Thankful for the invisible things we have received, we even begin to taste and savor them now: "O taste and see that the Lord is good!" (Ps. 34:8).

Less self. More God. "He must increase, but I must decrease" (John 3:30). Praise and thanks help make Him the focus. Feelings come and go; He remains always the same. Praise and thanks help Him become our focus as our own doubts dissipate like shadows before the light. Praise and thanks bring you to a blessed self-forgetfulness, to a blessed God-centeredness. Cling to Him. Lay hold of Him in faith, hope, and charity. Lean on Him. Cast yourself on Him. Find in Him that still point at the center of reality, that still point at the center of your soul. He is our all. He is what is most real: our Eucharistic Lord of Love enthroned on the altar. "The substance belongs to Christ" (Col. 2:17). All else not built on Him will pass away: Therefore, if any one is in Christ, he is a new creation; the old has passed away, behold, the new has come" (2 Cor. 5:17).

*Let Us Pray:* My God, my all, I acknowledge that it is all about You! It's certainly more about You than myself. Help me to live a God-centered existence. May Your truth reign in my mind and heart. And may Your steady faithfulness, goodness, and love be the solid rock on which my life is built.

## Today's Reflection

*What "ultimate reality" leaped out and grabbed*
*your attention in this meditation today?*

*"He must increase, but I must decrease." Ask*
*the Lord to show you the areas of your life where*
*you need a renewed vision, a renewed sense*
*of reality, to see things as He sees them.*

Day 27

# Bathed in His Presence
# and His Blood

*What is this Mystery which is all around me?*

—St. Gregory of Nazianzus

*He who dwells in the shelter of the Most High, who abides
in the shadow of the Almighty, will say to the LORD, "My
refuge and my fortress; my God, in whom I trust." ... He
will cover you with his pinions, and under his wings you
will find refuge; his faithfulness is a shield and buckler.*

—Ps. 91:1-4

The Lord's presence is a stronghold and a place of refuge for us.
The Lord's presence is a nurturing and consoling place of love.
The Lord's presence is even a light for the soul. In the presence of
God's love, our souls are filled with a new brightness. John Tauler,
O.P., speaks of the God who "lights up thy soul brilliantly with His
presence ... until all thy capacity for Him has been filled by His
blessed presence."[100] We experience all this in Eucharistic Adoration.

---

[100] John Tauler, "God Is Gained by Detachment from Creatures—Sermon for the First Sunday After Epiphany," in *Sermons and Conferences*, 118-119.

The Scriptures also speak of God's name in the same way as His presence. In the manifestation of who God really is, we abide in a stronghold. So, Jesus prays, "Holy Father, keep them in thy name" (John 17:11). Likewise, Zephaniah speaks of taking "refuge in the name of the Lord" (Zeph. 3:12). In that place of the truth of God's love, we are protected and nourished. When we perceive God as love, as faithful and true, we find rest and flourish. Moreover, in our recognizing the God who even now accomplishes His saving work for us, He is a strong tower for us. The Eucharist contains all this, as it is the Real Presence of the God of love and the summit of our redemption. Put differently, in Eucharistic Adoration, we are bathed in His presence and bathed in His Blood.

Jesus' blood shed for us shines forth with the truth of God's love for us. St. Catherine of Siena explains it in this way: "Who is Truth? God is supreme eternal Truth. In whom shall we come to know this Truth? In Christ, gentle Jesus, for with his Blood he has shown us the eternal Father's truth."[101] The truth of God, who He truly is, what His name is, is the God who is love. And the blood shed for us manifests this. So to bathe in God's presence, His name, and His saving work is to bathe in the blood. St. Thomas Aquinas takes up this theme in this verse of "Adoro Te Devote":

> Like what tender tales tell of the Pelican,
> Bathe me, Jesus Lord, in what thy bosom ran —
> Blood that but one drop of has the pow'r to win
> All the world forgiveness of its world of sin.

In Eucharistic Adoration, we are invited not only to behold the Sacred Mysteries but to be immersed in them. Hence Aquinas eloquently implores the Lord here, "Bathe me, Jesus Lord, in what

---

[101] *Letters of Catherine of Siena,* T193.

thy bosom ran—Blood that but one drop of has the pow'r to win." Within a century, another Dominican, St. Catherine of Siena, would make this an all-encompassing motif of her own. The Seraphic Mother, St. Catherine, continues to speak such words to us:

I long to see you bathed, immersed in the Blood of Christ crucified, and hidden in His open side. In the Blood you will discover fire (because it was shed for love), and in His open side you will find hearty love [a strong love]. For Christ shows that everything that He does in us is done with such hearty love. Then your soul will be set ablaze with a fire of holy desire, a desire that is an impulse of love.[102]

How do we become immersed in the Precious Blood of Jesus? Well, next to the precious but brief moments of Holy Communion, the most poignant way that we are immersed in the Blood is in Eucharistic Adoration. Christ is present in the Host, Body, *Blood*, soul, and divinity. Eucharistic Adoration is basically one long "spiritual communion" with our Eucharistic Lord. We are in communion with the Blood that we adore in Eucharistic Adoration. The love of God and the saving influence of God in the Blood covers us. We feel it penetrating every pore of our being as we abide with Jesus in the Eucharist and perceive His true name of Love. We genuflect as we enter the chapel, acknowledging that we have entered a sacred space where we are immersed in God's presence and immersed in His Blood. We are hidden in the open side of Jesus, hidden in His heart.

If it helps, you might ponder the round Host in the monstrance almost as if it is a round drop of Jesus' Blood. You might think of it as a drop of Jesus' Blood exerting its saving influence on you—making you white in the Blood of the Lamb as the Host

---

[102] *Letters of Catherine of Siena*, T158.

is already made white. Drops of Blood continue to flow from the heart of God as Hosts are distributed, one after another, during Mass—drop after drop of Blood flows fresh from the heart of God, still warm with the heartbeat of God. Such pious thought-exercises can help us to be immersed deeply in the Blood during Eucharistic Adoration. As we take in this Blood, blazing with the fire of God's love, it is as Catherine says: "Then your soul will be set ablaze with a fire of holy desire." Spiritually in communion with the strong, hearty love of God, seen in the Crucified One, we will have such a love stirred up in us. Then, as we come forth from the prayer furnace of the adoration chapel, the open side of Jesus, the fiery heart of Jesus, we too will set the world ablaze!

*Let us pray:* Lord, I come before You and bask in Your sheltering presence, Your peaceful presence, Your fragrant presence, Your anointed presence, Your presence thick with the Word, Your Abba-presence, Your life-giving presence, Your savory presence, Your overshadowing presence, Your presence that itself sheds light thick with love. Overshadow me with Your bright cloud (Matt. 17:5)! Bathe me in Your presence! Bathe me in Your Blood!

## Today's Reflection

*What line or phrase makes you most conscious
of the gift of God's presence?*

*"Drop after drop of Blood flows fresh from the heart
of God, still warm with the heartbeat of God."
How do you respond to this great mystery?*

Day 28

# High and Lifted Up

*I saw the Lord sitting upon a throne, high and lifted up;
and his train [of his robe] filled the temple. Above him stood
the seraphim. Each had six wings: with two he covered his
face, and with two he covered his feet, and with two he
flew. And one called to another and said: "Holy, holy, holy
is the Lord of hosts; the whole earth is full of his glory."
And the foundations of the thresholds shook at the voice
of him who called, and the house was filled with smoke.*

—Isaiah 6:1–4

What would we have seen if we were hidden away in a corner
when the prophet Isaiah experienced his vision of the Lord in
the temple? We probably would have seen with our physical eyes
just this: a humble man bowing down in reverence before the
invisible God. Then, after some back-and-forth with God, his face
suddenly lighting up as the prophet stands up with a new purpose
and mission from God. The scriptural account suggests that,
although the sublime reality was really present, it was a personal
vision for Isaiah alone, not for all those in the temple. As Isaiah
himself recounts it, it is not "*we saw,*" but "*I saw*" (Isa. 6:1). This

same lofty reality is also present in the Eucharistic Adoration chapel, perceived by each one of us through faith.

The reality that Isaiah describes is surely always there. Where the Lord is, He reigns in majesty surrounded by angels who sing night and day, "Holy, holy, holy!" The robe of his glory fills the space as the smoky and mysterious fragrance of love pierces and permeates our hearts. The objective reality is always there, but it was given to Isaiah on that day in the temple to see it. And seeing it changed the course of his life.

The Sacred Scriptures do not just give us information about things but they mediate reality to us. Moreover, the Scriptures mediate to us an encounter with the Lord. St. Gregory the Great observes that "the same Spirit of life that touches the mind of the prophet, touches the mind of the reader." As we read Isaiah, chapter 6, we are meant to be brought into a like encounter with the Lord, similar to what Isaiah experienced in the temple. There will be differences suited to our individual circumstances and God's call and will in our lives, but the basic core of the encounter is given to us through the inspired Word of God. This is all heightened as we bear that word in our heart before the Lord, high and lifted up, and enthroned in the monstrance in Eucharistic Adoration.

In Eucharistic Adoration, we too can perceive, with the eyes of faith, the Lord seated in majesty on His throne, high and lifted up, with the train of majesty filling the space of the chapel and the angels crying out, "Holy, holy, holy!" as the foundations of our existence shake before this transformative encounter with the Lord of Glory. Whereas Isaiah saw it with his physical eyes or the eyes of his mind, we tend to read this passage and just have a simple intuitive sense of this reality derived from faith. As we see other people kneeling before the altar in humble reverence, let us not miss the fact of what can be unfolding in their souls too, as we could have easily missed what was happening to Isaiah as he entered the temple in meekness and lowliness.

The angels sing their "Holy, holy, holy!" even into eternity (see Rev. 4:8). They are invisible but nonetheless really gathered around our Eucharistic Lord in the chapel. As you are naturally drawn to join in with a song that you hear others singing, so too the silent music of the angelic "Holy, holy, holy" ever so gently draws you into an attitude of reverence before our Eucharistic Lord.

In this holy space of the chapel, a holy space opens up in our souls. With "the eyes of [our] hearts enlightened" (Eph. 1:18), we perceive in faith the hidden God reigning in majesty under the appearance of simple bread. When our whole being acknowledges the majesty of the infinite God and the praise and self-oblation He so deserves, we are in a good place to receive our mission. It can be our mission for the day, for this season in our journey, or even our whole life vocation. We too can enter into the basic dialogue Isaiah had with the Lord: "And I heard the voice of the Lord saying, 'Whom shall I send, and who will go for us?' Then I said, 'Here I am! Send me'" (Isa. 6:8).

The encounter with the Lord turns into being sent to accomplish His will. Theophany, however sublime or simple it may be, leads to mission. Pondering the Word of God in the majestic presence of our Eucharistic Lord leads to receiving an anointed word we are meant to share with others, whether a whole congregation or someone close to our heart. God's revelation to everyone through the Scriptures becomes particularized into a message for our situation or the context of those to whom we are sent.

How could we be up to such a challenge of speaking a living word from the heart of God to the heart of our listeners? For Isaiah, it took a burning coal from Heaven that touched his lips.

For us, it will take the Eucharist, the Bread from Heaven, touching our lips and bringing us the Word-made-flesh, who is spirit and life and fire: "Then flew one of the seraphim to me, having in his hand a burning coal that he had taken with tongs from the altar. And he touched my mouth" (Isa. 6:6–7). The God who is "holy, holy, holy" is a consuming fire and a word, and He enters into us through the Eucharist. This allows us to accomplish what we could not on our own but that God sends us to do: "Here I am! Send me."

If we ever feel our words becoming more and more empty—maybe even as we speak more and more of them!—we need more time before Our Lord in Eucharistic Adoration. In the sacred silence that joins the silent music of the angelic "Holy, holy, holy," we find ourselves once again by that humble prophet who enters the temple and bows in reverence before the Lord of Glory, high and lifted up on His throne. "This the one whom I approve," the Lord says, "the afflicted one, crushed in spirit, who trembles at my word" (Isa. 66:2, NABRE). In this humble and pleading stance, we are able to receive an anointed word from the Lord, with the weight of His Eucharistic presence behind it as we share it. We can then answer our high and uplifting call: "Comfort, comfort my people, says your God. Speak tenderly to Jerusalem" (Isa. 40:1–2).

While the words of men, even our best-crafted ones, pass like the wind, "the word of our God will stand forever" (Isa. 40:8). This holy seed can sprout even in the desert and bring God's abundant life. As a result, the glory of the Lord will be seen in the temple (Isa. 6) and, from there, out into the world. "The wilderness and the dry land shall be glad, the desert shall rejoice and blossom; like the crocus it shall blossom abundantly, and rejoice with joy and singing. The glory of Lebanon shall be given to it, the majesty of Carmel and Sharon. They shall see the glory of the Lord, the majesty of our God" (Isa. 35:1–2).

*Let Us Pray:* I come to You, Lord, in humble faith. There are many stumps and barren lands before me. I come before You in the Eucharist to bow before Your majesty and open myself to a word that can save. Through Your presence and word, anoint me for the mission You give me anew each morning. Help me to radiate Your holiness, presence, and love throughout the land. Amen.

## Today's Reflection

*Imagine you are hidden away in a corner, and the Lord permits you to see the vision He gave Isaiah. What do you notice?*

*The Lord purified Isaiah with a touch of burning coal. How does this passage (Isa. 6:6–8) speak to you?*

Day 29

# Food of the Father's Will

*"What is it?" ... "It is the bread which*
*the Lord has given you to eat."*

Exodus 16:15

Today we will reflect on the relationship between the Eucharist as Holy Communion and the growth of our communion with God by following His will. Jesus declares to us today, "Do not labor for the food which perishes, but for the food which endures to eternal life, which the Son of man will give to you" (John 6:27). What is this food that endures into eternal life? It is life-giving communion with the will of the Father. In John 4, Jesus speaks of doing the will of the Father as food. "My food is to do the will of him who sent me and to accomplish his work" (v. 34). There is a heightened communion with the Father in doing His will, in living in His love. "The one who sent me is with me; he has not left me alone, for I always do what is pleasing to him" (8:29, NRSVCE). And this communion with God in carrying out His will is nourishment for us. In whatever God calls us to, we can cry out with the psalmist,

177

"I will never forget your commandments, for by them you give me life" (Ps. 119:93, NLT).

Doing the will of the Father is our food. His plan nourishes us as it becomes our purpose and single-hearted aim. I recall one morning receiving a phone call from my major superior informing me that St. Catherine's Priory in New York City had elected me as their prior. My initial reaction was a full-throated "What?!" I did not see that coming, and I saw how totally unfit I was for the position. God's will seemed too much for me. Then, later that day at Mass, I heard the reading from Exodus about the manna in the desert. "What is this?!" the Israelites exclaimed, put off by that bland-looking food. I then realized that I had reacted the same way to God's will. "What is this?!" Well, it is the Father's spiritual nourishment for me. It is His food for me because He would give me the grace to do His will, and our communion would be deepened by my heart being stretched by His will.

Doing God's will is not only our task to fulfill; it is also the food that nourishes us. The commitment of obedience, by laying ourselves open to the requirements of the Other, opens us to the rich abundance of the Other. The Father calls us to more, and this stretches us and gives us life as it breaks us out of our own narrow confines into "the breadth and length and height and depth" of God's love (Eph. 3:18). Work for this food that endures into eternal life.

What is this work? To believe in the one whom the Father has sent (John 6:29). This emphasis on belief highlights the relationship that is deepened by doing the Father's will just as Jesus, the one sent, does the Father's will. Doing the will of the Father with Jesus is about life-giving communion. It is about the relationship with the Father and the Son and also the Holy Spirit, who shows up in this passage in more subtle ways. Life-giving communion is brought about by the Holy Spirit. In fact, St. Augustine says life-giving Communion *is* the Holy Spirit. Jesus had already indicated this anointing that He, the Son of Man, bears: "For on him has God the Father set his seal" (John 6:27). The seal of the Holy Spirit stamps and binds the humanity of Christ to the Father who has sent Him. Doing the will of the Father and always pleasing Him is what this communion looks like in human life. This life-giving communion is opened to us as the Son, the true Bread of Life, comes down from Heaven to bring us into this life-giving communion: "For the bread of God is that which comes down from heaven, and gives life to the world" (John 6:33).

"I have come down from heaven, not to do my own will, but the will of him who sent me" (John 6:38). Jesus' whole purpose is doing what He was sent to do. Indeed, His whole identity is encompassed in being the one who is sent. This phrase is applied to Jesus throughout the Gospel of John almost as a title. And we too are taken up into this sending. We are sent in the Sent One as Jesus breathes the Holy Spirit into us. "'As the Father has sent me, even so I send you.' And when he had said this, he breathed on them, and said to them, 'Receive the Holy Spirit'" (John 20:21–22). The seal of the Holy Spirit stamps us and binds us to the One Sent and the One Who Sends as a communion of love. This life-giving communion with the Blessed Trinity is the food that will endure into eternal life and which we grow in by doing the will of the Father. This is the food that we labor for and endures into eternal life; that Jesus, the Bread of Life, has come down from Heaven to give us a share in.

When we go to Holy Communion in Mass or abide in the presence of the Bread of Life in Eucharistic Adoration, this communion of love is strengthened and nourished. The Son's communion with the Father in the Holy Spirit encompasses us. Our relationship to the Eucharist is trinitarian. Entering the church or the adoration chapel is entering more fully into the Trinity. Jesus, the Bread of Life, is present as the One Sent, drawing us into His own posture of open obedience. The Eucharist strengthens us to do the Father's will. God the Father is the one who sends, sending us on our particular mission for the day. And the Holy Spirit is that life-giving communion, encircling it all with the relationship of love. Gaze upon Jesus in the monstrance. Yet also see before your eyes the love of the Father who has given such a gift (John 3:16) and perceive the Spirit in the presence radiating forth and enveloping you.

When we find doing God's will difficult, therein lies a hidden call to come to the Eucharist. Come to the Bread of Life! It is His very existence to be the One Sent and He draws us into His own loving obedience. When we gaze into the Sacred Host, this dynamism sweeps us up into trinitarian love. And here, Jesus nourishes us with the Father's will and breathes into us the Spirit of life. We still labor, but now "for the food which endures to eternal life, which the Son of man will give to you" (John 6:27). The gift of the Eucharist leads us deeper into the will of God, deeper into the communion of love. Bring before our Eucharistic Lord your struggles in carrying out God's will, whatever they are, and in due time, you will find yourself sent in the Sent One, nourished, upheld, and ready to accomplish your share in God's work.

> *Let Us Pray:* Lord Jesus, You are the Bread of Life. Please nourish me with Your love and grace as I live out every dimension of my life in obedience to our loving Father in Heaven. Overshadowed by your Spirit, may I find His will to be more and more my food and nourishment. I

bear the yoke with You, Lord Jesus, so, as I give my yes in trust, I too declare that Your burden is bearable and Your yoke is sweet.

## Today's Reflection

*What line or thought draws your attention as you read?*

*"When we find doing God's will difficult, therein
lies a hidden call to come to the Eucharist."
When have you experienced this?*

Day 30

# Prophets from Mountaintops

*For the Lord had endowed Catherine of Siena with a
most ready tongue, a charisma of utterance adapted to
every circumstance, so that her words burnt like a torch
and none who ever heard her could escape being touched
by at least some spark of her burning eloquence.*

—Bl. Raymond of Capua[103]

We need prophets coming from the mountaintop more than
prophets coming from the marketplace. We need divine revelation
for the salvation of our souls. We need this from the beginning
to the end of our working out our salvation. Belonging to God
means belonging to Him more than to the world, and we can do
this only by being continually open to His word. The choice between God and the popular mentality of the world is decisive and
stark: "Anyone who chooses to be a friend of the world becomes
an enemy of God" (James 4:4, NIV). To whom do we belong:

[103] Bl. Raymond of Capua, O.P., *The Life of St. Catherine of Siena*,
trans. George Lamb (TAN Books, 2009), 9.

God or the world? Choosing to spend time in the Eucharistic Adoration chapel is a choice for God. It opens and strengthens us to accept His word even as it may contradict popular sentiment. And when we receive such a word, we have something to share with the world, something that the world does not already know. We have a living word to share that can bring salvation. Recall our meditation on Elijah a few days ago.

We have all had the experience: The more we are around worldly-minded people, the more we find their views becoming persuasive to us. And the more we are around devoted Christians, the more we find that their views ring true. But even more so, it is when we are around the Lord Himself in His Real Presence in the Eucharist that God's way of seeing things becomes our way of seeing things. Holiness means being set apart from the world. It means having a different way of seeing things than the rest of the world. Our moods shift depending on the company we keep. Praying before the presence of Jesus is a stronghold of truth. As a result, praying with the words of Scripture before our Eucharistic Lord is a place of prophetic insight.

To speak a prophetic word is not so much about foretelling something in the future. Prophecy is seeing the unfolding of history as God sees it. It is to be able to interpret what is happening from God's perspective. To speak a prophetic word is to speak into a situation a living word that manifests what God is up to and encourages the hearer to come into accord with and further God's plan. And His plan is at times rather unexpected. St. Paul describes the prophetic word like this: "One who prophesies speaks to people for their upbuilding and encouragement and consolation" (1 Cor. 14:3, ESV).

This is what the Old Testament prophets did, such as Isaiah. When Israel was led into the Babylonian captivity, Isaiah was sent by God to them with a message. If there had been a secular newspaper in their time, the newspaper would surely have just seen the exile in terms of political factors. But it is given to the prophet Isaiah to see the unfolding of Israel's history as God does. It is because of their lack of faithfulness to the Lord and His covenant that they are led to Babylon. And Isaiah does not leave them with this bad news but speaks words of good news into the situation as he proclaims God's promise of restoration and consoles the people as he encourages them with words of tender love and promise from the Lord (Isaiah 40-66).

Prophets—both from the past and today—need to be attentive to earthly circumstances, but it is really a word from above that the prophet awaits and delivers. Only thus is it a word that can save as it helps bring about God's plan. The Lord makes this clear to Isaiah: "For my thoughts are not your thoughts, nor are your ways my ways, says the Lord. For as the heavens are higher than the earth, so are my ways higher than your ways and my thoughts than your thoughts" (Isa. 55:8-9).

Every baptized person has a share in Christ's threefold office of priest, prophet, and king. We are all called to prophesy for others' "upbuilding and encouragement and consolation" (1 Cor. 14:3). Like Ezekiel, our prophetic word is to breathe new life into dry bones (Ezek. 37). We are to speak a living word that truly upbuilds and lifts people up to walk in God's ways, even as it is a word that sometimes pricks the conscience. To do this, we ourselves need to be radically attuned to Him by dwelling with Him. Being focused more on Him than on ourselves or the world, we belong to Him more than to ourselves and so can speak His word.

Praying before our Eucharistic Lord as we read the Bible helps us see things as God does. His Spirit touches our minds with His grace and He speaks within us. We are called to "let all mortal flesh keep silence … as the Light of light descendeth from the realms of endless day," as the famous Eucharistic hymn puts it. We need prophets who come from the mountaintops, from the place where our Eucharistic Lord is enthroned on the altar and enthroned in our hearts. It is then that, as St. Irenaeus puts it, "our way of thinking is attuned to the Eucharist," attuned to the Lord and His plan of salvation (quoted in CCC, no. 1327).

It is a refrain frequently repeated in the book of Revelation, as John delivers this prophetic word to the seven churches: "Let anyone who has an ear listen to what the Spirit is saying to the churches" (see 2:7, 11, 17, 29; 3:6, 13, 22). It is worth noting from whence these words come: John sees a strange figure moving among the lampstands, the seven lampstands which he informs us are the seven churches (Rev. 1:20). This mysterious figure is Jesus, and He is still the one among the lampstands of our churches today through His Real Presence in the Eucharist. John describes it like this:

> Then I turned to see the voice that was speaking to me, and on turning I saw seven golden lampstands,and in the midst of the lampstands one like a son of man, clothed with a long robe and with a golden sash around his chest. The hairs of his head were white, like white wool, like snow. His eyes were like a flame of fire, his feet were like burnished bronze, refined in a furnace, and his voice was like the roar of many waters. In his right hand he held seven stars, from his mouth came a sharp two-edged sword, and his face was like the sun shining in full strength. (Rev. 1:12–16, ESV)

Have you spent time realizing that this is the one we encounter in Eucharistic Adoration? He gazes back at us in love with "eyes like a flame of fire" and, as we read in the living and powerful Word of God, "His voice is like the roar of many waters" and it pierces our hearts beyond our worldly ways of thinking as "from his mouth comes a sharp two-edged sword" and His face shines like the sun. Spend some time in the Eucharistic Adoration chapel realizing who it is before you. Open the Bible to receive His living Word into your heart like streams of living water. Then look with love toward a person or situation that really needs the Lord and humbly ask for a living word that will upbuild, encourage, and console in the truth of the Lord.

> *Let Us Pray:* Lord, help me be a humble and bold prophet from the mountaintop of contemplation and prayer as I live out my baptismal call. Anoint me with a word of life for the world, especially for those entrusted to me. Give me, Father, a word of life that will further Your saving work today.

## Today's Reflection

*What line or phrase caught your attention in today's reading?*

*Reread the passage above about John's vision. Ask the Holy Spirit to reveal His word to you.*

Day 31

# Belonging Through Obedience of Faith

*With [his] life-giving gaze that produces saints, let us
beg for those Divine Glances that open the soul to holy
expansiveness. And let us allow ourselves to be bathed
in those Most Holy Glances that purify, sanctify, unite
and intimately bind the Divine Heart to our own.*[104]

—Bl. Concepcion Cabrera de Armida

Brothers and sisters, as we approach the end of our thirty-three-day
dedication, we will spend these next three days in the Scriptures
as a "Marian Triduum" of sorts, contemplating our Mother Mary
in light of the mystery of the Eucharist.

Our prayer belongs more to God than to us. So, when we
pray, we belong more to God than to ourselves. Eucharistic Adoration is a belonging to God that works from the inside out as
our prayer bubbles up within us from God as a share in His very
life. His life pulsates through us by grace and draws us to belong

[104] Bl. Concepcion Cabrera de Armida, *What Jesus Is Like*, ed. Con-
chita and Donald W. Montrose (Alba House, 2008), 40.

to Him even more. This happens in a way beyond what we could accomplish on our own. Abiding in the atmosphere of God's grace in Eucharistic Adoration draws us to belong more to the one who belongs to us.

We belong to God because He first gives Himself totally to us. "We love, because he first loved us" (1 John 4:19). Our response to this love is our obedience of faith. Responding to God's grace, we live out the obedience of faith in the return of our self-gift to God, as Vatican II puts it: " 'The obedience of faith' must be given to God as he reveals himself. By faith *man freely commits his entire self to God*, making 'the full submission of his intellect and will to God who reveals,' and willingly assents to the Revelation given by him."[105]

How do we best respond to this gift of God to us? With this obedience of faith, our yes to God. Mary did this best of all. "Behold, I am the handmaid of the Lord; let it be to me according to your word" (Luke 1:38). St. Paul's Letter to the Romans gives us the most theologically rich account of this obedience of faith and our belonging to God through justification by grace through faith. As we ponder the Letter to the Romans' teaching on justification, we should keep in mind Mary, who is a model for us in living out this obedience of faith.

The term "obedience of faith" frames St. Paul's Letter to the Romans, almost as bookends, at the beginning and end of the letter (1:5, 16:26). Misreadings of Romans that speak of "faith alone" miss this point that Paul makes so clear at the beginning and end. St. Paul, like a good writer, begins and concludes with his main point. And Paul's main point here is the obedience of

---

[105] Vatican Council II, Dogmatic Constitution on Divine Revelation *Dei Verbum* (November 18, 1965), no. 5.

faith, a faith that entails works. This obedience of faith flows from a more foundational belonging to God. The theme of "belonging" is also a fundamental way to appreciate this teaching on justification (being in a right relationship with God). To be justified is to belong to God.

St. Paul strives "to bring about the obedience of faith for the sake of his name among all the nations, including yourselves who are called to *belong* to Jesus Christ" (Rom 1:5–6, emphasis added). Indeed, Paul had already highlighted this belonging to Christ in the first line where he identifies himself as "a slave of Christ Jesus" (1:1, NABRE). St. Paul returns strongly to this theme in chapter 6, almost as another way to think about justification after chapters 3 and 4, which lay out key elements of this doctrine. Paul observes that we are either slaves to sin or slaves to obedience and righteousness (6:16–23). No longer slaves to sin but "slaves of God," we belong to God; this is His gift to us (6:22–23).

Paul then uses the image of marriage, where husband and wife belong to one another until one of them dies. In a similar way, "you have died to the law through the body of Christ, so that you may *belong* to another, to him who has been raised from the dead in order that we may bear fruit for God" (7:4, emphasis added). Dead to sin and no longer under the condemnation of the law, we belong to Christ. (Paul's Letter to the Galatians also depends heavily on this "belonging" language to elaborate on the doctrine of justification by faith, as in Gal. 1:10; 3:27, 29; 5:4, 24.) We can put it this way: Justification or being in right relationship with God is more about belonging than doing. It is through belonging to Christ that His righteousness is communicated to us by grace through faith (Rom. 3:21–26). This belonging is first brought about through Baptism (see 6:3–4).

While St. Paul captures this belonging to Christ in calling himself a "slave of Christ," Our Lady makes the same point about belonging to God by speaking of herself as "the handmaid of the Lord" (Luke 1:38). St. John Paul II emphasizes Mary's obedience of faith in his encyclical *Redemptoris Mater*. He builds on Vatican II's document *Lumen Gentium*, which presents Mary as the model of faith, hope, and charity. Mary is not simply an external model, but through her maternal mediation she helps us interiorly to respond with our obedience of faith to God. As St. John Paul II says, "In Mary's faith, first at the Annunciation and then fully at the foot of the Cross, an interior space was reopened within humanity which the eternal Father can fill 'with every spiritual blessing.' It is the space 'of the new and eternal Covenant,' and it continues to exist in the Church."[106]

Mary helps us to say yes to God even when it stretches our faith and tests our obedience, in order that we might belong to God and His plan even more completely. The obedience of faith is not only about us first being brought into a right relationship with God. It is also about how we live in perfect accord with God and His plan day by day. In other words, it is about how we belong to God in response to His grace day after day.

We can highlight three aspects of this obedience of faith.

+ First, acknowledging our humble poverty of spirit. As we grow in self-knowledge, our recognition of our need for God and for a Savior increases.
+ Second, admitting our neediness and weakness. So long as we bring him our "vessel of trust," in the words of St.

---

[106] Pope John Paul II, Encyclical on the Blessed Virgin Mary *Redemptoris Mater* (March 25, 1987), no. 28.

Faustina, these things need not be obstacles to God's plan but can be occasions for God's merciful love to be glorified. Our trust, or faith and hope, allows God's grace to penetrate into our situations of dire need.

+ Third, putting forth effort so our true mettle may be tested. In this way, we see better the real extent of our need. But it is also effort that allows God's grace to work through our whole being and life in the obedience of faith.

We can see these three elements of the obedience of faith lived out by Mary. In the Annunciation, Mary first humbly recognizes her lowliness, "Behold, I am the handmaid of the Lord" (Luke 1:38). Next, despite her littleness, she brings the Lord the vessel of her trust: "Let it be to me according to your word" (1:38). She does not understand how God's plan will be accomplished in the little she can bring to the table, yet she trusts. Finally, we see Mary putting her faith in action as she makes haste in going to serve her cousin Elizabeth (1:39-40). She lives out her faith and brings Jesus to others through her good deeds. As a result of her fiat, she sings her Magnificat (1:46-55).

In Eucharistic Adoration, we gaze upon God's complete gift of self to us and are drawn to belong to Him more completely through our obedience of faith. However difficult may be our fiat and yes to the Lord, we know that sooner or later it will prepare the way for our Magnificat and Eucharistic praise and thanks to God.

*Let Us Pray:* Lord, help me belong totally to You. Inspire me with the obedience of faith, that like Mary I may open the depths of my heart for Your word. Help me follow You in all things. Jesus, help me model my life according to the way You give yourself totally in the Eucharist.

## Today's Reflection

*On this first day of the "Marian Triduum," what strikes you about Mary's example of obedient trust?*

*Which of the three elements is most difficult for you, and how might God be calling you to change this?*

Day 32

# Mary's Immaculate
# Heart Will Triumph

*O Most Holy Trinity, Father, Son and Holy Spirit,
I adore Thee profoundly. I offer Thee the most
precious Body, Blood, Soul and Divinity of Jesus
Christ present in all the tabernacles of the world, in
reparation for the outrages, sacrileges and indifferences
by which He is offended. By the infinite merits of the
Sacred Heart of Jesus and the Immaculate Heart
of Mary I beg the conversion of poor sinners.*

—The Angel's Prayer at Fatima[107]

In her apparitions in Fatima, Portugal, in 1917, Our Lady of
Fatima proclaimed, "My Immaculate Heart will triumph." Why
is her Immaculate Heart specified? Why is it not just that Mary

---

[107] This is the prayer taught to the three children by the Angel of
Peace in 1916. See Caroline Perkins, "The 5 Prayers Revealed at
Fatima That Every Catholic Should Know," EWTN Great Britain,
May 12, 2025, https://ewtn.co.uk/chpop-the-5-prayers-revealed
-at-fatima-that-every-catholic-should-know/.

will triumph but that her *Immaculate Heart* will triumph? Well, it suggests that the real victory is interior, a victory of the heart.

In 2000, as prefect of the Congregation for the Doctrine of the Faith, then-Cardinal Joseph Ratzinger (the future Pope Benedict XVI) opened up the meaning of this phrase: "The Heart open to God, purified by contemplation of God, is stronger than guns and weapons of all kinds."[108] In a similar vein, Fr. Thomas McGlynn, O.P., who interviewed the visionary Sr. Lucia about the central meaning of the messages of Fatima, noted that the visionary insisted that the most important thing about the messages was not Russia but that the real focus was supernatural. And this supernatural core of Our Lady of Fatima's message is just as relevant in our own day.

What does it mean for Mary's Immaculate Heart to triumph? Mary's pure heart points to the fact that she was free of all sins of sensuality. It also points to her great purity of intention. Purity of heart is to will one thing: God's will. This is expressed in Mary's fiat. She is pure availability to God. She gives her complete unbounded yes to the Lord: "Behold, I am the handmaid of the Lord, let it be to me according to your word" (Luke 1:38). The victory of Mary's Immaculate Heart is interior. It is her drawing us into her yes so that we too can give to the Lord a yes that is complete and unreserved. When we give our yes, her Son is free to extend His Kingdom further into the world through us. Her Immaculate Heart triumphing is the opening of hearts for the reign of her Son to be extended in the world

---

[108] Cardinal Joseph Ratzinger, "Theological Commentary" on Congregation for the Doctrine of the Faith, *The Message of Fatima* (May 13, 2000), https://www.vatican.va/roman_curia/congregations/cfaith/documents/rc_con_cfaith_doc_20000626_message-fatima_en.html.

today. What Mary said at Cana continues to beckon us: "Do whatever he tells you" (John 2:5). This is her Immaculate Heart triumphing. And when we give her Son our unbounded yes, He loves to turn the water of our human efforts into the new wine of the Kingdom.

The supernatural focus of the call of Our Lady of Fatima can perhaps best be summarized in these maternal yet awe-inspiring words of hers: "Pray, pray very much and make sacrifices for sinners; for many souls go to Hell, because there are none to sacrifice themselves and to pray for them."[109] Part of belonging to the Lord is offering ourselves in love as a living sacrifice to Him for His glory and the salvation of souls. A belonging to God that does not involve some kind of penance or self-oblation is not authentic. Souls are counting on us, as Mary's weighty words remind us. God knows we do not like the Cross. So in His paternal tenderness, God gives us Mary at the foot of the Cross to help us make the offering as she did. The Cross is still the Cross, but Mother Mary sweetens it somehow. And she draws us into her own yes at the Cross. And her Immaculate Heart triumphs as we are joined to the offering of her Son, Jesus.

Our Lady of Fatima's call to offer prayer and sacrifice is actually even more specific than this, and this is key. The call is not simply to pray and make sacrifices but rather to "Pray, pray very much and make sacrifices." There is quite a big difference between the call to pray and to "Pray, pray very much." This is a repeated call from Our Lady in a number of apparitions. Each

---

[109] Apparition of August 15, 1917; George Pollard, "The Revelation of the Immaculate Heart at Fatima in 1917," EWTN, accessed July 3, 2025, https://www.ewtn.com/catholicism/library/revelation-of-the-immaculate-heart-at-fatima-in-1917-5465.

person must discern what precisely this call entails in their own particular circumstances: three hours of prayer daily, five hours, seven hours … What does it mean to pray, pray very much in each of our vocations? The call to pray, pray very much almost by definition will strike the half-hearted person as excessive. But it is only in praying very much that we can come to love the Cross and find joy in it as Mary sweetens it and draws us into her own pure availability for the Lord and His purposes.

Through her relationship with Mary and her Son, Sr. Lucia later in life could exclaim, "O Will of God, you are my paradise!" Mary's Immaculate Heart had triumphed in Sister Lucia's heart. We see this unfolding in a scene from Lucia's life when she was much younger. In the midst of facing persecution and suffering in bearing witness to the apparitions amidst much suspicion and doubt, Our Lady of Fatima consoled Lucia as she does us today too: "Does this cause you to suffer a great deal? I will never leave you. My Immaculate Heart will be your refuge and the way that will lead you to God."[110] Our Lady wants to show herself a mother in our lives and let her gentle and sweet Immaculate Heart triumph over our fears and resistance. This drama is often played out in the Eucharistic Adoration chapel as we gaze upon our Eucharistic Lord and occasionally glance in the direction of a beautiful statue of Our Blessed Mother. Jesus has given Mary to us as a mother precisely to help us in these ways.

Other famous words from Fatima are significant here. This call to "pray, pray very much" means not only petitionary prayer

---

[110] John de Marchi, I.M.C., The True Story of Fatima: A Complete Account of the Fatima Apparitions (1947; repr., Fatima Center, 2009), 25, https://fatima.org/wp-content/uploads/2017/03/The-True-Story-of-Fatima.pdf.

but also includes adoration and a laying down of everything at God's feet in love. At the heart of the Fatima message is a call to make reparation in Eucharistic Adoration. In 1916, the "Angel of Peace" appeared to the three children at Fatima and taught them to pray over and over again: "My God, I believe, I adore, I hope and I love Thee! I ask pardon for all those who do not believe in Thee, do not adore Thee, do not hope in Thee, do not love Thee!"[111]

The prime setting to enter into this reparatory adoration is the Eucharistic Adoration chapel, as things unfold deeply over time and in silence. In this prayer of reparation for those who do not adore, we stand in their place and adore the Lord on their behalf. Sometimes the most significant thing we can do for a loved one for whom we are praying is to adore the Lord on their behalf. Our petitionary prayer and silent adoration for them can return their souls to Christ and make them His again.

In the silent stirrings of love in Eucharistic Adoration, we enter into pure adoration of God, forgetting self and all the things we want from God, moving from the gifts to the Giver. We enter into a selfless adoration of God, being caught up in Him, more focused on Him than ourselves and drawn into the pure availability that was also in Mary's Immaculate Heart. It is all about the Lord God! This movement of adoration brings our belonging to God to a new level. Mary's Immaculate Heart triumphs in drawing us into her own limitless yes all the more. As you kneel before the Lord in Eucharistic Adoration, let Mother Mary's influence wash over you and let yourself be drawn to that place of purity of heart where it is all about God. There, Mary's Immaculate Heart triumphs and our Eucharistic Lord is enthroned in our hearts.

[111] De Marchi, *True Story of Fatima*, 98.

*Let Us Pray:* Heavenly Father, pour out into my heart the Spirit of prayer and self-offering. May I make my life a ceaseless prayer of desire for You. Give me a desire to make reparation in Eucharistic Adoration for all the great evils that offend Your heart and for the conversion of sinners. Use my life to contribute to the triumph of Mary's Immaculate Heart.

## Today's Reflection

*What stood out to you in today's reflection?*

*On whose behalf is the Lord asking you to make reparation? What form is that reparation to take, that Mary's Immaculate Heart may triumph?*

Day 33

# "The Woman in the Desert"

*God's temple in heaven was opened, and the ark of his covenant
was seen within his temple. There were flashes of lightning,
rumblings, peals of thunder, an earthquake, and heavy hail.
And a great sign appeared in heaven: a woman clothed with
the sun, with the moon under her feet, and on her head a crown
of twelve stars. She was pregnant and was crying out in birth
pains and the agony of giving birth. And another sign appeared
in heaven: behold, a great red dragon, with seven heads and ten
horns, and on his heads seven diadems. His tail swept down a
third of the stars of heaven and cast them to the earth. And the
dragon stood before the woman who was about to give birth, so
that when she bore her child he might devour it. She gave birth
to a male child, one who is to rule all the nations with a rod of
iron, but her child was caught up to God and to his throne, and
the woman fled into the desert, where she has a place prepared
by God, in which she is to be nourished for 1,260 days.*

—Revelation 11:19–12:6, ESV

We have come to the last day in our pilgrimage to dedication day
tomorrow. Hopefully these days of savoring God's word is stoking your desire for our Eucharistic Lord. We begin today with

turning the eyes of our heart to the last book of the Bible and this mysterious woman in the desert.

Who is this woman of Revelation 12? Is she Israel? Is she Mary, the Mother of Jesus? Is she the Church? Good Catholic scriptural exegesis has no problem saying with assurance: She is all three! The Scriptures are rich like that, often having a polyvalent and multi-layered meaning. Before circling back and considering this woman in terms of the new Israel, the Church, and how we stand with Mary in this place of intercession, some explanation is required in seeing the woman as Mary.

Catholic theology observes that Mary did not suffer birth pangs in giving birth to Jesus, since labor pains are a result of original sin, from which Mary was preserved. What are these birth pangs then? They are what we could call "eschatological birth pangs." Eschatology refers to the "last things," the final state of affairs when Christ's redeeming work will be brought to its fullness and all the redeemed will attain "to mature manhood, to the measure of the stature of the fulness of Christ," and will "grow up in every way into him who is the head, into Christ" (Eph. 4:13,15).

There are pangs involved in coming to full maturity in Christ, and Mary's maternal mediation helps bring this about. Mary experienced these eschatological "birth pangs" at the foot of the Cross as she consented to the awful suffering and death of her Son and as she became the mother of all the disciples of Jesus. "Woman, behold, your son!" "Behold, your mother" (John 19:26–27). And through Mary's maternal mediation, she continues to help Christ come to full maturity in the soul of every Christian. What St. Paul says, Mary can say all the more: "My little children, with whom I am again in travail until Christ be formed in you!" (Gal. 4:19).

The woman of Revelation 12 is our Blessed Mother. And yet the Church, the new Israel, also shares in this same mission along with Mary. The Church, as mother, gives birth to new Christians in the baptismal font. As a mother, she helps Christians grow to full maturity through all the sacraments and the day-to-day nourishment of Word and Sacrament. We as members of the Church also help bring Christ to full maturity in His members in the Mystical Body of Christ. We do this in concrete acts of service to our neighbor, but we also do this in the offering of ourselves for others in the desert place of contemplation.

An important detail about the woman of Revelation 12 is that she is brought to the place of the desert. The desert in the Bible is the place of being stripped of all extraneous things and brought into an essential encounter with the Lord. The Lord beckons His beloved people into the desert: "Therefore, behold I will allure her / and bring her into the wilderness, / and speak tenderly to her" (Hos. 2:14, RSV). Israel is tested in the desert and Moses encounters the Lord on the mountain top in the desert (Exod. 19). Elijah also travels through the desert to meet the Lord on the mountaintop in the still, small voice (1 Kings 19). Jesus Himself spends his early morning hours withdrawing into the desert to pray (Luke 5:16).

Hence, when God prepares a place for the woman of Revelation 12, this whole biblical background of the desert is evoked. It is the desert place of contemplation where we find the woman in her role of maternal mediation. And it is when we stand fast in the arid place of the desert in prayer that we have a profound share in Mary's intercession and maternal mediation. There are pains involved in remaining faithful to a life dedicated to prayer, and it helps to recognize them as part of the eschatological birth pangs of the Church and our Blessed Mother. We share in Mary's own maternal mediation when we stand strong in this place of intercession.

Sometimes the Eucharistic Adoration chapel is a prayer furnace. Sometimes it is a desert of aridity in prayer. Sometimes it is a place of anguish. But through it all, our Blessed Mother is with us, interceding. She is not simply praying for us but also drawing us up into her own intercession for the Church and the accomplishment of the plan of her Son. The early Desert Fathers went into the desert to enter into spiritual combat with the evil one and, into our own day, the desert remains a place of spiritual combat. And our victory is in Jesus.

The angels sing a song in Revelation 12 about the slain Lamb's triumph over all opposed to God: "Now the salvation and the power and the kingdom of our God and the authority of his Christ have come, for the accuser of our brothers has been thrown down, who accuses them day and night before our God. And they have conquered him by the blood of the Lamb and by the word of their testimony" (Rev. 12:10–11). Our victory comes through the blood of the Lamb and the word of testimony. More particularly, our victory comes through the Eucharist (Christ's true Body, *Blood*, soul, and divinity) and the Scriptures, the Word of God. Blood and Bible. Sacrament and Word. Before our Eucharistic Lord with the Bible open in our hands—this is our place of triumph.

The time is short. One way or another, our days on earth are short. They are a time of birth pangs bringing to full maturity the new man in Christ Jesus. John, the author of Revelation, recounts in his Gospel a similar image of the woman giving birth. Right before it, he records Jesus' words about it being just "a little while" until we will see Him again. It is no mistake that the phrase "a little while" is repeated precisely seven times, the perfect, eschatological number (John 16:16–19). For, among other meanings, Jesus' words here have an eschatological ring to them as well; it is an *eschatological little while*: "A little while, and you will not see me, and again a little while, and you will see me" (16:17).

Tomorrow, eternity. It will come more quickly than we probably realize, in just a little while. Our birth pangs for the Kingdom of Christ will find ample recompense in just a little while. "When a woman is giving birth, she has sorrow because her hour has come, but when she has delivered the baby (*paidion*), she no longer remembers the anguish, for joy that a human being (*anthropos*) has been born into the world" (John 16:21, ESV). We reach out past this little while in the Eucharistic Adoration chapel, which is so often a desert place of contemplation and self-offering. There, in the midst of birth pangs in company with our Blessed Mother, we hasten the full coming of the Kingdom of Christ. We become ever more our true selves in Christ.

*Let Us Pray:* Lord, draw me more deeply into the cry of the Spirit and Bride: Come! Come, Lord Jesus! (Rev. 22:17). Fill me with the same compassionate Spirit that fills Mother Mary's heart! Draw me more deeply into her maternal intercession as I share in the birth pangs and groanings of all creation (Rom. 8:22–23). Fill it all with your love! Make me Yours, Lord.

## Today's Reflection

*Hopefully these thirty-three days created a little desert time in your life to sit and listen deeply to the saving truths of our Catholic Faith. Fr. Jesse and I pray it opened up some desert spaces for contemplation. Hopefully it encouraged you to seek the Lord's face in the Eucharist with new zeal and love. We pray that in the desert spaces of Eucharistic Adoration Christ brought you ever more deeply into Himself. Our hope is you have become more His.*

# Dedication Day

In his Sermon 38, St. Augustine says that "our whole business … in this life is to heal the eye of the heart whereby God may be seen."[112] As we have journeyed these thirty-three days through so many truths that touch on the reality of the living presence of Jesus in the Most Holy Eucharist, we pray that the eyes of your heart are now more open to the great mystery of the Eucharist. May our minds and hearts be totally attuned to a Eucharistic way of life. May the Eucharistic presence of Christ no longer be merely an idea or notion but rather a truly lived experience. Hopefully this journey has been one of renewal in a greater intensity of love for our Eucharistic Lord. After these weeks are over, may we all grow in our sense of how much the Father desires and draws us to Jesus in order to be drawn up ever more into the life that they share in the Holy Spirit.

What are we going to do now with all this knowledge and experience in which we have grown during these days? How are we going to become missionary disciples of our Eucharistic Christ?

[112] St. Augustine, "Sermon 38 on the New Testament," no.5 at *New Advent*, https://www.newadvent.org/fathers/160338.htm.

How are we going to become agents of right reverence and worship of our Eucharistic Lord? Will we be better prepared for Mass? Will we promote and keep silence in Church when it is appropriate? Will we dedicate more time to thanksgiving after Mass? Will we visit the tabernacle or a Eucharistic Adoration chapel more often? Will we be like St. Andrew and go out and call others to "come and see" Jesus in the Eucharist? What are the fruits of this thirty-three-day journey for you, and how are you going to ask the Lord to help you mature in them? In your dedication, you form the resolution, with the help of God's grace, to give yourself more frequently and more fervently in devotion to the Eucharist. Such a resolution is a holy one, and it is helpful to ask a friend or relative or fellow parishioner to hold you accountable to it. Only then can we really bring about the change the Church needs so badly, so the Eucharistic Christ can be the light on the hill for all to see.

As you make your dedication today, you can write and pray your dedication in your own words or you can use the optional prayer that we have provided. Whatever you do, ask the Lord to give you the grace to fulfill your dedication all the days of your life as best you can.

Brothers and sisters, Jesus longs for you to be His. He awaits you in the Holy Eucharist to transform you ever more into Himself. He longs to bind you into an even deeper union with Himself. Just let Him love you. Show up and He will do the rest! Let us dedicate ourselves!

# Prayer of Dedication

*(Optional)*

Heavenly Father, I dedicate myself today to Jesus Christ Your Son, my brother, my friend, and my Lord, in the Most Holy Eucharist. In the presence of the Blessed Virgin Mary my mother, and St. Joseph and all the saints and angels, I entrust my life to an ever-greater devotion to the Most Holy Eucharist. I dedicate myself to greater reverence and love to our Eucharistic Lord. I firmly resolve to attend Holy Mass more frequently and to make more time for Eucharistic Adoration in a spirit of reparation and love for souls. Lord Jesus, help me remove all obstacles that prevent me from sitting at Your feet in love and adoration. Give me the zeal to call others to adore and worship You in adoration.

Lord Jesus, bind me to Your Eucharistic Heart, and may I feel the fire of Your love and the light of Your wisdom. Burn away in me all falsehood and produce in me a true likeness of Yourself. I want to be Yours. Teach me. Prompt and guide me. Help me hear the desire and longing in Your heart for my love. Make me a Eucharistic Apostle of Your love.

# Prayers and Litanies

*Litany of the Most Blessed Sacrament*
By St. Peter Julian Eymard

Lord, have mercy. R. Lord, have mercy.
Christ, have mercy. R. Christ, have mercy.
Lord, have mercy. R. Lord, have mercy.
Christ, hear us. R. Christ, graciously hear us.

God the Father of Heaven, R. Have mercy on us.
God the Son, Redeemer of the world,
    R. Have mercy on us.
God the Holy Spirit, R. Have mercy on us.
Holy Trinity, one God, R. Have mercy on us.

Jesus, Eternal High Priest of the Eucharistic Sacrifice,
    R. Have mercy on us.
Jesus, Divine Victim on the Altar for our salvation,
    R. Have mercy on us.
Jesus, hidden under the appearance of bread,
    R. Have mercy on us.

Jesus, dwelling in the tabernacles of the world,
    R. Have mercy on us.
Jesus, really, truly and substantially present in the
    Blessed Sacrament, R. Have mercy on us.
Jesus, abiding in Your fulness, Body, Blood, Soul
    and Divinity, R. Have mercy on us.
Jesus, Bread of Life, R. Have mercy on us.
Jesus, Bread of Angels, R. Have mercy on us.
Jesus, with us always until the end of the world,
    R. Have mercy on us.

Sacred Host, summit and source of all worship and
    Christian life, R. Have mercy on us.
Sacred Host, sign and cause of the unity of the Church,
    R. Have mercy on us.
Sacred Host, adored by countless angels,
    R. Have mercy on us.
Sacred Host, spiritual food, R. Have mercy on us.
Sacred Host, Sacrament of love, R. Have mercy on us.
Sacred Host, bond of charity, R. Have mercy on us.
Sacred Host, greatest aid to holiness,
    R. Have mercy on us.
Sacred Host, gift and glory of the priesthood,
    R. Have mercy on us.
Sacred Host, in which we partake of Christ,
    R. Have mercy on us.
Sacred Host, in which the soul is filled with grace,
    R. Have mercy on us.
Sacred Host, in which we are given a pledge of
    future glory, R. Have mercy on us.

Blessed be Jesus in the Most Holy Sacrament of
　　the Altar, R. Have mercy on us.
Blessed be Jesus in the Most Holy Sacrament of
　　the Altar, R. Have mercy on us.
Blessed be Jesus in the Most Holy Sacrament of
　　the Altar, R. Have mercy on us.

For those who do not believe in Your Eucharistic
　　presence, R. Have mercy, O Lord.
For those who are indifferent to the Sacrament of
　　Your love, R. Have mercy on us.
For those who have offended You in the Holy
　　Sacrament of the Altar, R. Have mercy on us.

That we may show fitting reverence when entering
　　Your holy temple, R. We beseech You, hear us.
That we may make suitable preparation before ap-
　　proaching the Altar, R. We beseech You, hear us.
That we may receive You frequently in Holy Commu-
　　nion with real devotion and true humility,
　　R. We beseech You, hear us.
That we may never neglect to thank You for so
　　wonderful a blessing, R. We beseech You, hear us.
That we may cherish time spent in silent prayer
　　before You, R. We beseech You, hear us.
That we may grow in knowledge of this Sacrament
　　of sacraments, R. We beseech You, hear us.
That all priests may have a profound love of the
　　Holy Eucharist, R. We beseech You, hear us.
That they may celebrate the Holy Sacrifice of the
　　Mass in accordance with its sublime dignity,
　　R. We beseech You, hear us.

That we may be comforted and sanctified with
    Holy Viaticum at the hour of our death,
    R. We beseech You, hear us.
That we may see You one day face to face in Heaven,
    R. We beseech You, hear us.

Lamb of God, You take away the sins of the world,
    R. Spare us, O Lord.
Lamb of God, You take away the sins of the world,
    R. Graciously hear us, O Lord.
Lamb of God, You take away the sins of the world,
    R. Have mercy on us, O Lord.

V: O Sacrament Most Holy, O Sacrament Divine,
R: All praise and all thanksgiving be every moment
    Thine.

*Let Us Pray:*
Most merciful Father, You continue to draw us to Yourself
through the Eucharistic Mystery. Grant us fervent faith in
this Sacrament of love, in which Christ the Lord Himself
is contained, offered, and received. We make this prayer
through the same Christ our Lord. R. Amen.

### *Prayer Before Mass*
#### By St. Thomas Aquinas

Almighty and ever-living God,
I approach the sacrament
of Your only-begotten Son
Our Lord Jesus Christ,
I come sick to the doctor of life,
unclean to the fountain of mercy,

blind to the radiance of eternal light,
and poor and needy to the Lord
of heaven and earth.

Lord, in Your great generosity,
heal my sickness,
wash away my defilement,
enlighten my blindness, enrich my poverty,
and clothe my nakedness.

May I receive the bread of angels,
the King of kings and Lord of lords,
with humble reverence,
with the purity and faith,
the repentance and love,
and the determined purpose
that will help to bring me to salvation.

May I receive the sacrament
of the Lord's Body and Blood,
and its reality and power.

Kind God,
may I receive the Body
of Your only-begotten Son,
our Lord Jesus Christ,
born from the womb of the Virgin Mary,
and so be received into His mystical body
and numbered among His members.

Loving Father,
as on my earthly pilgrimage
I now receive Your beloved Son

under the veil of a sacrament,
may I one day see Him face-to-face in glory,
who lives and reigns with You for ever.
Amen.

### *Prayer of Thanksgiving After Mass*
#### By St. Thomas Aquinas

Lord, Father all-powerful and ever-living God, I thank You, for even though I am a sinner, Your unprofitable servant, not because of my worth but in the kindness of Your mercy, You have fed me with the Precious Body & Blood of Your Son, our Lord Jesus Christ.

I pray that this Holy Communion may not bring me condemnation and punishment but forgiveness and salvation.

May it be a helmet of faith and a shield of good will.

May it purify me from evil ways and put an end to my evil passions.

May it bring me charity and patience, humility and obedience, and growth in the power to do good.

May it be my strong defense against all my enemies, visible and invisible, and the perfect calming of all my evil impulses, bodily and spiritual.

May it unite me more closely to You, the One true God, and lead me safely through death to everlasting happiness with You.

I pray that You will lead me, a sinner, to the banquet where You, with Your Son and holy Spirit, are true and perfect light, total fulfillment, everlasting joy, gladness without end, and perfect happiness to your saints.

Grant this through Christ our Lord. Amen.

# What's Next? Resources to Continue Your Journey

by Dan Burke

If you have made it this far, it is certain that you have found this book a powerful resource to help you come to know and encounter the Lord in ways you likely had not thought possible. Now you might be wondering: How can I go deeper? Are there other resources that emanate from the same spiritual well from which this book was drawn?

Here are a few resources we recommend for the deepening of your quest to know and come to union with God:

**SpiritualDirection.com/His**: Here you will find short video reflections by Fr. Jesse Maingot on each chapter of this book. These will help you on days when reading is less desirable, or just to add additional perspective for your consideration and prayer.

**DominicanHouseofPrayer.com** (DHOP): DHOP is a house of studies for the soul. This web site offers homilies, conferences, and brief discussions on various topics related to Catholic spirituality and devotional practice in its YouTube channel and retreats online and on site. Here you will also find more from Fr. Jesse Maingot and Fr. Ignatius Schweitzer.

May God bless you as you continue this journey into the Sacred Heart of Christ!

# About the Authors

Fr. Jesse Maingot, O.P., is a Dominican priest of the Irish Province, currently stationed in Trinidad and Tobago. He was ordained in 2019. Fr. Jesse completed his S.T.L. in dogmatic theology at the Angelicum University in Rome. He has a heart for rebuilding the culture of worship and adoration of Our Eucharistic Lord. Currently Fr. Jesse is the promoter for Eucharistic Adoration in the Archdiocese of Port of Spain. He also teaches there in the seminary of St. John Vianney and the Ugandan Martyrs. He was recently appointed by Pope Francis as a Missionary of Mercy.

Fr. Ignatius John Schweitzer, O.P., is a Dominican priest of the Province of St. Joseph. He is the Director of Spiritual Formation and a professor at St. Joseph's Seminary in Dunwoodie, and the provincial promoter of the Lay Dominicans. He lived as a Carthusian monk from 2012 to 2018 and, in some ways, has never left the desert. He feels his particular mission is helping people grow in the spiritual and mystical life. He is a co-author of the book *Named for Glory: St. Elizabeth of the Trinity's Identity and Mission*, published by Sophia Institute Press.

DAN BURKE is the founder and president of the Avila Institute for Spiritual Formation, which offers graduate and personal enrichment studies in spiritual theology to priests, deacons, religious, and laity in more than ninety countries and prepares men for the seminary in more than one hundred dioceses. Dan is the author or editor of more than fifteen books on authentic Catholic spirituality. To learn more, visit SpiritualDirection.com or ApostoliViae.org.

# Sophia Institute

Sophia Institute is a nonprofit institution that seeks to nurture the spiritual, moral, and cultural life of souls and to spread the gospel of Christ in conformity with the authentic teachings of the Roman Catholic Church.

Sophia Institute Press fulfills this mission by offering translations, reprints, and new publications that afford readers a rich source of the enduring wisdom of mankind.

Sophia Institute also operates the popular online resource CatholicExchange.com. *Catholic Exchange* provides world news from a Catholic perspective as well as daily devotionals and articles that will help readers to grow in holiness and live a life consistent with the teachings of the Church.

In 2013, Sophia Institute launched Sophia Teachers to renew and rebuild Catholic culture through service to Catholic education. With the goal of nurturing the spiritual, moral, and cultural life of souls, and an abiding respect for the role and work of teachers, we strive to provide materials and programs that are at once enlightening to the mind and ennobling to the heart; faithful and complete, as well as useful and practical.

Sophia Institute gratefully recognizes the Solidarity Association for preserving and encouraging the growth of our apostolate over the course of many years. Without their generous and timely support, this book would not be in your hands.

www.SophiaInstitute.com
www.CatholicExchange.com
www.SophiaTeachers.org

Sophia Institute Press® is a registered trademark of Sophia Institute.
Sophia Institute is a tax-exempt institution as defined by the
Internal Revenue Code, Section 501(c)(3). Tax ID 22-2548708.